LEON J. WARSHAW, M.D., F.A.C.P.

Equitable Life Assurance Society of the United States/New York

MANAGING STRESS

ADDISON-WESLEY PUBLISHING COMPANY

Reading, Massachusetts
Menlo Park, California • London
Amsterdam • Don Mills, Ontario • Sydney

This book is in the
Addison-Wesley Series on Occupational Stress

Consulting Editor: Dr. Alan A. McLean

Library of Congress Cataloging in Publication Data

Warshaw, Leon J
  Managing stress.

  (Occupational stress series)
  Bibliography: p.
  Includes index.
  1. Work--Psychological aspects. 2. Stress (Psy-
chology) 3. Psychology, Industrial. I. Title.
II. Series.
HF5548.8.W29   658.38'2   79-11187
ISBN 0-201-08299-9

Third Printing, March 1984

Copyright © 1979 by Addison-Wesley Publishing Company, Inc. Philippines copyright 1979 by Addison-Wesley Publishing Company, Inc.

ISBN 0-201-08299-3
CDEFGHIJK-AL-8987654

FOREWORD

The vast literature concerned with the individual coping with work stress stems from many and diverse disciplines, primarily psychiatry, clinical and social psychology, sociology, cultural anthropology, and occupational and internal medicine, with significant contributions from such widely different fields as behavioral toxicology and personnel and management. While each discipline is concerned with so-called "psychosocial stressors," communication between the several disciplines has generally been the exception rather than the rule. Lawyers, for example, tend to communicate mainly with other lawyers about the issues that concern them. Union leaders tend to communicate most often with other union leaders. Clinical psychologists direct their communications to their colleagues, but use a different language from that used by many of the psychiatrists who are equally concerned. Even social psychologists and industrial sociologists sometimes find it difficult to exchange data. The transfer of useful data from one discipline to another has proven to be very difficult. "Some researchers go about rediscovering the known, with little deference to an existing literature or to determinable frontiers for contemporary research; and what consensus may be possible is *not adequately disseminated for beneficial application beyond home base.*"*

---

* Robert Rose, editorial, *Journal of Human Stress*, Vol. 3 No. 1, March 1977.

Communication across disciplines is not the only difficulty that students of job-related stress encounter. Transcultural communication is a problem too. Western physiologists, for instance, who are concerned with hormones in the brain, have difficulty communicating with their eastern European colleagues who prefer to speak in terms of "higher nervous function."

There is growing common concern. Theories and practices in each discipline are beginning to cross-pollinate other disciplines and to exert a positive influence toward understanding the stresses of the workplace and workers' reactions.

The many denominators of concern for an employee population under stress form the unifying theme of these volumes. As a field of study, occupational stress is beginning to gel. It is a subject of increasing interest not only to members of unions and management, but also to the health professionals who serve as their consultants. Increasingly, awareness and expertise are being focused on both theoretical and practical problem solving. The findings of social scientists have led to the enactment of legislation in the Scandinavian countries, for instance, where employers are now required, under certain circumstances, to provide meaningful work and appropriate job satisfaction with a minimum of occupational stress.

The authors of these books represent many points of view and a variety of disciplines. Each, however, is interested in the same basic thing—greater job satisfaction and greater productivity for each employee. The books were written independently with only broad guidelines and coordination by the editor. Each is a unique, professional statement summarizing an area closely related to the main theme. Each extracts from that area applications which seem logically based on currently available knowledge.

All of the authors treat, from differing perspectives, three key concepts: stress, stressor, and stress reactions. *Stress* defines a process or a system which includes not only the stressful event and the reaction to it, but all the intervening steps between. The *stressor* is a stressful event or stressful condition that produces a psychological or physical reaction in the individual that is usually unpleasant and sometimes produces symptoms of emotional or physiological disability. The *stress reaction* concerns the consequences of the stimulus provided by a stressor. It is, in other words, the response to a stressor, and it is generally unhealthy. Most often, such reactions may be defined in rather traditional psychological terms, ranging from mild situational anxiety and depression to serious emotional disability.

Many frames of reference are represented in this series. A psychoanalyst describes the phenomenon of occupational stress in executives. A sociologist reflects the concern with blue-collar workers. Health-care-delivery systems and the prevention of occupational stress reactions are covered by occupational physicians. Other authors focus on social support systems and on physiological aspects of stress reactions. All the authors are equally concerned with the reduction of unhealthy environmental social stimuli both in the world of work and in the other aspects of life that the world of work affects. In each instance, the authors are concerned with defining issues and with drawing the kinds of conclusions that will suggest constructive solutions.

The legal system, beginning with worker's compensation statutes and more recently augmented by the Occupational Safety and Health Act, deals directly with occupational stress reactions and will be the subject of one of the books in the series. That statute, which created both the Occupational Safety and Health Administration and the National Institute for Occupational Safety and Health, contains a specific directive mandating study of psychologically stressful factors in the work environment. We have seen criteria documents and standards for physical factors in the work environment. We may soon see standards developed to govern acceptable levels of psychological stressors at work such as already exist in Sweden and Norway; another significant area of concern for this series.

At the beginning of this series it is difficult to foresee all the pivotal areas of interest which should be covered. It is even more difficult to predict the authors who will be able and willing to confront the issues as they emerge in the next few years. In a rapidly changing technological, scientific, and legislative world, the challenge will be to bring contemporary knowledge about occupational stress to an audience of intelligent managers who can translate thoughts into constructive action.

Alan A. McLean, M.D.
Editor

PREFACE

This book is intended to help managers on all levels to recognize, appreciate, and control stressors in the workplace and to develop and operate stress-management programs that will relieve their adverse effects on individual workers and/or the work organization. The intent is not to make therapists or social scientists out of business people, but to explain what such professionals can offer and to help the organization derive greater benefits from their activities in the work setting. It is not intended to be a "do-it-yourself" guide to mental and emotional health, although it may provide information and insights that will point ways toward self-improvement. It does not pretend to be encyclopedic or the "last word," but it offers a distillation of current knowledge and past experience that will serve as a framework for more searching exploration of specific problems as they arise. Finally, it represents a strenuous effort to minimize technical terminology and professional jargon and to avoid entrapment in the arenas of ideologic and philosophic controversy.

I want to persuade readers of this book that, since stress is an inevitable part of every work organization, the vitality and viability of the organization and their success as managers depend on their ability to recognize stress, to understand its effects, and to control its impact. The art and science of management is essentially the definition of the organization's mission, the establishment of its goals and objectives, the recognition of conflicting variables, the selection of the most advantageous alternatives, and the measurement of results. But all this must be done within the constantly changing contexts of technological development, economic fluctuations, social expectations, and government regulation. And it can be accomplished only through people interacting and cooperating with each other, individually and in groups. Problems arise when individuals, groups, or entire organizations find themselves in roles in which they do not fit, or are forced to withstand levels of stress with which they cannot cope. The management of stress requires the anticipation and prevention of these problems and, since that is not always possible, their prompt recognition and correction.

In the chapters that follow, I will examine the sources of stress in the work setting and how stress affects the organization and its personnel. I will consider the various kinds of programs and activities that can be undertaken to ameliorate the effects of stress on individuals, groups, and the organization as a whole. Above all, I hope the reader will focus on incorporating an appreciation and understanding of stress and the ability to deal with it effectively into the art of management.

I will draw on the scientific literature which is growing at an exponential rate and on the expertise and wisdom of the medical and social scientists who have made—and continue to make—significant contributions to this field. The content of the book will also reflect the experience and perceptions of managers in a wide variety of work organizations in this country and abroad.

In addressing this book to managers, it may appear to separate those who manage from those who are managed. That there is a difference is epitomized by the Hollywood motion picture executive who is reported to have said, "I don't get ulcers; I give ulcers!" The special world of the executive is described in a companion volume.* Here, it is taken for granted that managers are also workers, people to whom stress is important not only in terms of their own well-being, but also because its impact on their judgment and decisions will affect many others and the organization as well. This book will be considered successful if, rather than creating stress for managers by giving them additional items to be concerned about, it helps them to appreciate the true significance of their role and to perform it more effectively.

---

*Moss, L. (1979). *Executive Stress*. Reading, Mass.: Addison-Wesley.

It is not feasible to identify and acknowledge each item I have drawn from other individuals. Suffice it to say that no claim for originality is made for any part of this book while the author takes full responsibility for the opinions and recommendations it offers.

I am deeply grateful to Alan A. McLean, valued friend and esteemed colleague, whose foreword opens this book. He not only conceived this series on Occupational Stress, but while carrying more than a full burden of professional and extracurricular responsibilities, found the time for an incisive page-by-page critique of this manuscript. He deserves a good part of the credit for any virtues this book may possess.

I am indebted to a number of individuals for their generous expenditures of time and energy in reviewing the manuscript in its various stages of preparation and for their most helpful comments and suggestions. They include: David L. Bertelli, Jan Bryn, Richard Egdahl, Rosalind Hawley, Robert Katz, Hans Kraus, Morton Miller, Preston K. Munter, Harris T. Schrank, Bernard Schuman, Celia Ussak, and Joan Waring.

I am grateful to Josephine Giglio, Rutha Holley and their staff at the Equitable's word-processing unit for their skillful nurturing of the manuscript, and to Charles T. Peers, Jr., and Barbara Pendergast for handling so well the complexities of its publication.

Finally, I wish to acknowledge in print my deep appreciation to my wife, Mona, for her support and her forbearance throughout the undertaking that this book represents.

New York, New York   L. J. W.
May 1979

CONTENTS

PART I
STRESS IN THE WORK SETTING

1

INTRODUCTION

Stress is a major problem in the contemporary United States. It negatively affects the daily lives of scores of millions of Americans. It causes a bewildering array of physiological, psychological and social malfunctions. On an economic level, the effects of stress probably cost the nation over $100 billion annually. Moreover, available evidence suggests that stress-related maladies are on the rise.

(MITCHELL, 1977, p. vi)

Although this conclusion, reached by Arnold A. Mitchell in one of a series of studies commissioned by the Director of the National Science Foundation in his role as Presidential Science Advisor, may sound to the reader like hyperbole, it is, in fact, a gross understatement. Stress affects the lives of all people, everywhere. It is a cause of illness and accidents, producing stress in the victims, those who must care for them, and those who care about them. Stress affects personality, modifying our perceptions, feelings, attitudes, and behavior. And it reaches beyond its immediate victims to affect the political, social, and work organizations whose activities they direct and carry out. And these organizations, as living, functional entities, are also affected by stress: Their growth and survival are very much related to their success in coping with stress.

The cost of stress is incalculable. Health economists have yet to find a generally acceptable method of calculating the value of a day of disability or of years of life lost to premature death. Courts are required to place dollar values on "pain and suffering," but no one pretends that these have any validity; they are not even consistent. We can estimate the costs of waste of materials and imperfect products or services, but how accurately can we distinguish between shoddy merchandise and the expected erosion of wear and tear? And how do we distinguish the results of faulty judgment and bad decisions from the consequences of unavailable knowledge and bad luck?

Stress has generated an immense conglomerate of business enterprises. A major portion of the health-care industry, second in size only to government—which for many is a major cause of stress—deals with stress. Vast entertainment and recreation industries help people to cope with stress, and the travel and vacation industries help people to escape from it. In such industries as the media and the arts, stress is a raw material to be fashioned into books like this one, and people like me, consultants and teachers, try to help people and organizations prevent or ameliorate its effects. Finally, do not forget the scientists in the varied disciplines who are working hard to measure and understand the actions of stress and to contrive better ways to control them.

I agree with Mitchell that stress-related maladies are on the rise. Part of that rise, however, is apparent rather than real. Such illnesses have always plagued us, but they have been ascribed to a variety of causes or simply labeled "idiopathic"—that is, "the cause is not known." Now, thanks to our growing knowledge of the anatomy, chemistry, and physiology of human functions, we are beginning to appreciate the pathogenic role of stress.

Part of the increase in stress-related maladies reflects changes in our definitions and concepts of "sickness" and "health." The new concepts of "wellness" are epitomized in the World Health Organization's declaration that health is more than the absence of disease. We now speak of the "quality of life" and reach for "self-actualization" and "fulfillment" while we strive to control factors that can impair not only physical but also psychosocial well-being. Thus, part of Mitchell's increase results from a shift in the boundary between health and disease so that much of what used to be considered a "normal" part of human existence is now regarded as a deviation from health that should be treated or, better still, prevented.

Nevertheless, much of the increase Mitchell describes is real. It reflects the increasingly rapid and complex changes that have taken place in the world during the past half century. It is a much more crowded world, thanks to its rising population, faster, more commodious means of transportation, and more effective techniques of communication. Profound changes in political, economic, and cultural institutions and dramatic modifications of social values, such as our evolving concepts of human rights, accompanied by the mixed blessings of our new scientific knowledge and technology signalize what we have come to call the "postindustrial era."

In the work setting, Mitchell's conclusions are no less applicable than in the global scene he was studying. Stress is a major problem in work organizations throughout the industrialized world. It affects workers on every level and manifests itself in terms of absenteeism, reduced work output and poor work quality. It leads to inefficiency and waste and to costly impairment of relationships within and outside the organization.

A brochure advertising self-development courses in the management of stress states, "In the business world, stress seems to be the number one by-product of success. There's no escaping it . . ." That may be, but in my view, stress is also the hallmark of failure: failure of the individual in his or her work and/or in his or her personal life—and failure of the organization as well.

ORGANIZATIONS AND THE MANAGEMENT OF STRESS

Why should an organization care about its ability to manage stress in the work setting? The simplistic answer is that its productivity and viability depend on its people and how well or how badly they perform.

But it is, of course, more than that. The transition of the advanced industrial societies into the "postindustrial era" has been accompanied by massive changes. Consider the events of the past few decades: continuing technological development, wars, political upheavals, the emergence from colonialism of the developing countries, and most of all, the bruising experience of inflation. Manufacturing, the foundation of the Western economic system since the Industrial Revolution, is being replaced as the major source of employment by service industries and government. Youth are rebelling against staid authority and traditional institutions. Minorities have demanded and are winning equality and respect. Workers are refusing to take jobs that they perceive as wanting in dignity and personal satisfaction. (In industrialized countries, these jobs are being filled by nationals of the less-developed areas to whom these jobs represent an upward social move.) Increasing numbers of young people and many who have already achieved measures of success are "opting out," electing to "escape from the rat race" and return to a "simpler life." Workers are demanding shorter weeks and longer vacations and many are retiring early.

At the same time, there have emerged new patterns of social behavior, altered priorities, and new values. Work for its own sake is acquiring a different—some say less important—position in our scale of values, and the lure of material possessions is losing its potency, at least for those who already have them or ready access to them. The objectives of workers have shifted gradually from achievement and control to self-actualization and self-expression. The hierarchy of command can no longer expect automatic respect or blind conformity to authority. More and more, workers are demanding participation and involvement in decision making. The trend toward centralization in both industry and government has been reversed by a movement toward "regionalization" and smaller local units with increasing autonomy in determining their own priorities in allocating resources. Here, as well as abroad, growing numbers of organizations are being introduced to concepts of social responsibility by government and the courts and forced increasingly to fulfill the needs of their workers and their customers and to conform to emerging social principles.

In this context, then, the management of stress becomes essential to the continuing maturation and long-term viability of the organization.

There are also more mundane reasons. Health authorities and governments seeking to halt the escalation of health-care expenditures are emphasizing with increasing vigor and effectiveness the role of stress and unhealthy patterns of behavior in the genesis of the chronic "diseases of civilization" and are urging the adoption of life-styles that will lessen their impact. Similarly, organizations alarmed by the rising cost of employees' health and disability benefits are mounting health education and promotion programs and, at the same time, paying more attention to the possibility of preventing the adverse health effects of work and the workplace. These activities are also being mandated by new and more demanding government regulations relating to employee health and safety.

Labor unions are becoming more aggressive in their drive to force employers to stop their exploitation of workers' health and upgrade work that is dehumanizing. Following the examples of Norway and Sweden, they are demanding a greater participation of workers in decision making, not only in the design and structure of the job and work practices, but in the management of the organization as well.

The history of the American labor movement and its struggles over the past century and a half amply justifies the unions' inherent mistrust of management and their desire to retain control over any advances earned by them for their members. It explains their seeming paranoia in perceiving any unsolicited expressions of management interest in worker welfare as a ploy to court the affection of their employees and undermine their loyalty to the union (Morris, 1978).

And yet, there appears to be ample reason to raise similar questions of vested self-interest about the behavior of some unions. Many union leaders appear to regard the traditional adversarial relationship with management as essential to their survival. Exploitation of members on a grand scale by a number of unions has been disclosed in the public press and I have had personal experiences in which the welfare of a union member was sacrificed on the altar of rigid adherence to rules and precedents. Too often, the objective of a campaign against stressful and unhealthy working conditions has appeared to be not to secure the safety and well-being of the workers, but to win them special privileges and increased "hazard" pay. Similarly, the real objective of efforts to shorten the work week has been not to provide workers more time for rest, relaxation, and the pursuit of recreational activities, but to increase the amount of overtime at premium pay and provide a greater opportunity for moonlighting, often in a second job in the same industry.

My point here is not to "put down" the unions but to emphasize the legitimacy of suspicion on both sides of the bargaining table and to decry the concept that either can claim a monopoly of concern about worker welfare. I would urge the replacement of "win-lose" contests by mutually respectful collaborations. There are already many situations in which this has occurred and their number is increasing, but there is still a long way to go.

The threat of increasing claims for worker compensation benefits is another defensive reason for management to be interested in stress.

It has been proven that workers under stress are more likely to have accidents. It should be noted that the inattentiveness and boredom evoked by the stress of underload are also liable to cause accidents and, further, that while the stressed worker may cause the accident, the victim who suffers the injury may be a coworker or some other innocent bystander.

The courts have declared stress to be a precipitating cause of such catastrophic events as a heart attack or a stroke for which sizable monetary benefits have been awarded. Such cases have usually been based on evidence of an acute crisis at work, a heated argument, an overzealous "dressing down" by a superior, or some other incident in which a work-related stressor appeared to rise suddenly to an unusual level. A new theory, first accepted in California and now recognized in several other jurisdictions, holds that such chronic conditions as coronary artery disease, cancer, stroke, and end-stage hypertensive kidney disease can be caused by the cumulative effect of repeated or continuous exposure to work stressors over an entire career. When such claims are successful, the last employer of record may be financially responsible for all of the benefits or they may be apportioned among all of the employers listed in the individual's work history, depending on the law in the particular jurisdiction.

We all as individuals have a responsibility for our own health which we cannot pass on to others. There is no longer any room for the "old-fashioned" kind of nurturing paternalism which, however it was rationalized, was often a way of exercising control over an organization's work force. What the organization is responsible for is to create and maintain a physical, emotional, and social environment that will preserve and enhance the health and well-being of its workers, or at least avoid their impairment. Failure to do this leads to worker discontent and illness, which are expressed in absenteeism, high turnover, low productivity, poor work quality, and even deliberate sabotage. I would emphasize, however, that the basic reason for managing stress in the work setting is to help the organization to survive and flourish in the emerging postindustrial era.

In casting about for some meaningful way to epitomize the soaring significance of stress in our era, I am reminded of the comment made some years ago in Hollywood by Samuel Goldwyn, the world-famous producer of motion pictures and renowned master of malaprop and nonsequitur. Rushing into the set in his studio and interrupting the filming of a scene from *The Apartment*, he waved the front page of the afternoon paper at the members of the cast and crew who gathered around him. Pointing to the large picture of the mushroom cloud over Eniwetok produced by the first hydrogen bomb explosion and struggling to share his awe at the significance of that event, he asked, "What do you think of that?" He then answered his own question by shouting, "It's dynamite!"

And so it is with stress: "Dynamite!" Ever present, ever potent, as simple and yet as complicated as a human being, made by humans, inflicted on humans, and controllable by humans.

REFERENCES

Mitchell, A. (1977). *The Effects of Stress on Individuals and Society.* Menlo Park, Calif.: The Stanford Research Institute, No. 77-206.

Morris, R. B., ed. (1978). *The American Worker.* Washington, D.C.: U.S. Dept. of Labor (No. 029-000-00256-8).

2

WHAT IS STRESS?

The influence of stress in the development of illness has been recognized for centuries but it is only during the past fifty years that we have gradually come to appreciate its significance and begun to understand how it works.

The methodical investigation of stress began in the 1920s with the classic observations of William B. Cannon and other physiologists of the bodily changes produced by emotions. As a result of their work, scientists began to appreciate the importance of hormones and chemical mediators in the body's reactions to its internal and external environments. With advances in scientific technology and instrumentation, this understanding continues to advance.

During the early 1930s, under the leadership of the renowned Chicago psychoanalyst Franz Alexander, and Flanders Dunbar at Columbia's College of Physicians and Surgeons in New York, observations of the relationship between distinctive personality patterns and "constitutional" tendencies to certain organic disorders led to the development of the "psychosomatic" theory of disease. In oversimplified form, this theory holds that the way we are put together and our long-established patterns of emotional response and behavior predispose us to particular types of illness.

In a letter to the editor of *Nature,* Hans Selye (1936) introduced his concept of stress as the "general adaptation syndrome," a set of physiologic reactions induced by a broad variety of environmental agents. Selye defined stress as the "nonspecific response of the body to any demand" and a stressor as an agent which produces stress at any time. Even stressors that have a specific localized effect will, if their magnitude is sufficient, cause the general, nonspecific stress reaction.

Stress reactions are not necessarily bad, Selye emphasizes. In fact, they cannot be avoided, since just being alive involves continuing response to internal and external stressors. Depending on their intensity and the way they affect the individual, these reactions can be helpful and even pleasurable. On the other hand, when they are insufficient, excessive, or inappropriate, discomfort and disease may result. Such ill effects can occur as a response either to continued exposure to the same stressor or to cumulative, collective exposures to a variety of unrelated stressors.

Selye's formulation popularized the concept of stress and initiated a wave of research and discussion that is still accelerating. It has occupied medical, behavioral, and social scientists around the world and over the last forty years has produced over 110,000 scientific articles, books, and reviews. There is an ever-growing number of topical subheadings in the computers of MEDLARS (Medical Information Literature and Retrieval Service) under which one may search for articles dealing with specific aspects of stress. And this body of scientific literature is dwarfed in comparison to the attention paid to the implications and applications of the stress concept in the media directed at the general public.

Although the frontiers of our knowledge of stress and its effects are expanding in all directions, we do not yet have all of the answers. There is a multiplicity of theories and unvalidated explanations, and the looseness with which terms are defined and used is compounded by the jargon indigenous to each of the individual scientific disciplines involved. All of this has generated some confusion and misunderstanding but, it can be said, there is general acceptance of the concept of stress as a description of the individual's reactions to environmental demands and influences and as an explanation of how external events influence individuals and populations. Stress is now accepted as a factor in the onset of any chronic disease, not just those designated as "psychosomatic." As Dodge and Martin (1970) put it, "stress is a product of specific socially structured situations inherent in the organization of modern technological societies."

Two developments of recent decades have added relevance to our growing knowledge of stress: the concept of "risk factors" and changes in the definitions of health and disease.

Risk factors are genetic, physiological, and behavioral characteristics that influence an individual's susceptibility to a particular illness. Groups of individuals with these characteristics show a greater incidence of the disease. It is important to note that not every member of a risk group will develop the disease, but it certainly will occur more frequently than in a group that lacks these characteristics. If the risk factors are eliminated in time (i.e., before any permanent effect is produced), the incidence of the disease will drop down to the level encountered in "normal" populations. Again, it is important to note that not everyone who does not have these characteristics will escape the disease, although they will be less likely to get it.

Changing definitions of health and disease have had a profound impact on our perceptions of the importance of stress. The earlier medical model focused only on illness and disease. While physicians attempted to control stress, their purpose was to prevent it from causing or aggravating disease. The newer, broader definition of health as more than the absence of disease forces us to become more concerned about the effects of stress on general well-being, behavior, and performance. It focuses attention on tension, anxiety, dissatisfaction, frustration, and unhappiness, not only as stressors which can cause adverse effects, but in their own right as departures from health as a positive state of "wellness."

It is important to emphasize that stress is defined here as the response to a stressor, a stimulus, or a set of circumstances that induces a change in the individual's ongoing physiological and/or psychological patterns of function. It is an inevitable and necessary part of living, as useful as the changes in breathing, heart rate, blood circulation, and metabolism evoked by physical activity as the stressor. Complete freedom from stress is death. Stress presents difficulty when the response is inadequate, inappropriate, or excessive or so prolonged that it exhausts the individual's capacity to respond. The difficulty may be expressed in emotional distress, aberrant types of overt behavior, or symptoms of illness, most commonly those associated with disorders of the nervous, cardiovascular, gastrointestinal, and respiratory systems. Unless addressed properly and relieved, such disorders will act as stressors in their own right and compound the stress.

Whether a particular stressor will produce difficulty or modify the individual's susceptibility to the effects of other stressors depends on the nature of the stressor and its magnitude or intensity, the vulnerability of the individual to its effects at that time, and the context or circumstances in which the stressor and the vulnerability are interacting.

The stressor may be a demand for physical activity or an environmental exposure to such potential toxins as heat, vibration, noise, radiation, dusts, or chemicals. It may be an emotional difficulty that produces distorted perceptions of ordinary circumstances or the psychological impact of such significant life events as the loss of a child or a spouse. Psychosocial stressors may be presented by one's status and role in the family and in the community, and as we shall see in the next chapter, stressors may arise out of an individual's work and the interpersonal relationships it involves.

Many investigators have attempted to isolate and quantify the relationships between particular stressors and the levels of stress they produce. The physiologic monitoring of graduated exercise tests on treadmills or bicycle ergometers provides fairly accurate measures of the cardiovascular or pulmonary stress induced by physical exercise, and the new discipline of behavioral toxicology is developing a technology to measure the stressor effects of low-level exposures to chemicals on brain and nervous functions. About ten years ago, Holmes and Rahe (1967) developed a forty-two-item "Schedule of Recent Experiences" in which they asked research subjects to evaluate the items in terms of importance and severity. From this, they developed a scale in which they rated the probability that the stress produced by these life changes would be associated with the onset of disease. The magnitude of the stress, they found, was correlated with the seriousness of the disease.

Paykel et al. (1971) repeated this study with an enlarged list of sixty-one items and subjected their subjects' scores to refined statistical analysis. The most potent stressors, they found, were death of a child, death of a spouse, a jail sentence, an unfaithful spouse, major financial difficulty, and business failure, in that order. Being fired ranked eighth, while being unemployed for at least one month ranked fifteenth. Other job-related factors such as demotion, arguments with a boss or coworker, change in career, change of work conditions, and relocation were well down the list, well below such items as onset of menopause or taking an important examination. This tends to confirm the prevailing impression that stressors in the work situation are much less potent than those encountered in personal life.

But these are merely statistical correlations. Not everyone exposed to the most potent stressors will develop a stress-related difficulty. (They would, however, certainly be more susceptible to the additive effects of stressors in the work situation or elsewhere.) These studies demonstrate that such rating scales are, at best, only crude estimates of the relative potency of stressors among selected samples of subjects. Even among them, the scores showed great variation, thus validating the truism that "one man's meat is another man's poison."

It is important, therefore, to avoid the trap of stereotyping stressors and the stress they produce. One type of reaction may produce increased effectiveness in one individual and difficulty in another. Symptoms sometimes indicate an increase in the intensity of a workplace stressor. Or, they may result from a constant exposure to that stressor at a time when the individual's vulnerability is increased by the effects of stressors in his or her home life. Or, the symptoms can result when both stressor and vulnerability are constant but unrelated concurrent changes in an individual's psychosocial environment modify his or her perceptions of the circumstances or block the support structures that ordinarily enable him or her to cope.

From the standpoint of the organization, it matters only that when stress impairs work performance it can often be relieved by neutralizing any one of a number of stressors or simply by helping the individual to cope with them more effectively. Analysis of one's particular constellation of stressors is indicated, but it will generally be found that those arising in the work setting are more accessible and amenable to intervention. This, combined with the opportunity to prevent problems by actions that eliminate such stressors or keep them from gaining intensity, is the fundamental rationale for an effective stress-management program.*

REFERENCES

Dodge, D., and W. Martin (1970). *Social Stress and Chronic Illness*. Notre Dame, Ind. University of Notre Dame Press.

---

* For a more detailed discussion of the dynamics of stress the reader is referred to two companion volumes in this series, Alan A. McLean's *Work Stress* and Lennart Levi's *Occupational Stress: Sources, Management, and Prevention*.

Holmes, T.H., and R.H. Rahe (1967). The social readjustment rating scale. *J. Psychosomatic Research* **11**:213–218.

Paykel, E.; B. Prusoff; and E.H. Uhlenhut (1971). Scaling of life events. *Arch. Gen. Psychiat.* **25**:340–347.

Selye, H. (1936). A syndrome produced by diverse nocuous agents. *Nature* **138**:32.

3
STRESS IN THE WORK SETTING

In order to comprehend fully the genesis of stressors in the work setting, we need first to examine what work means to the individuals who will be affected by stressors. Most social scientists agree that work fulfills a number of basic human needs and that failure to satisfy these needs or a perceived threat to their satisfaction represents the fundamental source of stress in the work setting.

1 *Maintenance.* Work provides the material goods essential for survival—directly for the self-sufficient pioneer or the refugee from modern civilization who would return to "basics," or indirectly for most of us by earning the money needed to buy them.

2 *Activity.* Even when their basic maintenance needs are satisfied, people seem to need some kind of regular, purposeful physical or mental activity.

3 *Social needs.* Most people seem to need the companionship and feeling of belonging that is derived from the human contacts in the work place.

4 *Self-esteem.* We need a sense of our own identity, a recognition of the value of what we have to offer and attainment of the rank to which we feel entitled. The absence of this is epitomized in comedian Rodney Dangerfield's tag-line, "I don't get no respect around here!"

5   *Self-actualization.* The sense of satisfaction that comes from developing competence and mastery in "doing one's own thing" is derived from the opportunity for growth and the realization of one's own potential.

It is obvious that work does not always meet all of these needs. Furthermore, the needs are not constant. Not only do they shift in relative importance over time, but the individual's perception of their magnitude and what it takes to meet them also changes. As a rule, these changes are in the direction of increased expectations: There seems to be an almost inexorable tendency for the need to grow as the individual comes close to satisfying it.

One particularly potent stressor that cuts across all of these needs is the lack of a job or the imminent threat of its loss. A number of observers have reported that economic downturns causing a rise in unemployment are accompanied by an increased incidence of symptomatic mental illness. Dr. Sidney Cobb, formerly director of the Mental Health in Industry program at the University of Michigan's Institute for Social Research and now professor of community medicine and psychiatry at Brown University, together with Dr. Stanislav V. Kasl of Yale, recently reported the results of a long-term prospective study of the physical and emotional health of workers at two plants that were being shut down. The emotional changes included a sense of deprivation, a loss of self-identity, and depression. A variety of physical symptoms were reported; these were more prominent during the period of anticipating the shutdown than after it occurred. There was an increase in arthritis and hypertension, and three men developed patchy baldness. There was also evidence of an increased frequency of peptic ulcers both in the men and their wives. In addition, laboratory data indicated an increase in risk factors for coronary heart disease, diabetes, and gout (Cobb and Kasl, 1978).

Some years ago, I observed similar reactions among the employees of a company soon after it was taken over by a large conglomerate. The new masters dispatched a cadre of young M.B.A.'s to examine the structure and functions of each department. As a result, whole units were eliminated or consolidated and a number of "old-timers" who had long ceased to be productive were let go. This was done in a systematic, orderly fashion that took over a year to complete. During that time, anticipation of "the axe," fed by news of each dismissal and "grape-vine" rumors about who would be next, produced waves of anxiety that permeated the atmosphere. Uncertainty, helplessness, and frustration led to depression and withdrawal in some employees and to irritability and anger in others. Visits to the Employee Health Department and absenteeism increased not only for minor complaints but also for such serious illnesses as coronary heart disease, ulcers, colitis, and arthritis. Counseling in coping with stress became a major activity.

It should be noted that decompensation (a difficulty that prevents normal performance) was no less frequent among employees who were judged to have been working productively than among those ultimately designated as redundant. From the standpoint of the organization, their disability, disaffection, and outright loss through resignations represented a significant portion of the costs of the "housecleaning" that might have been saved had it been planned and executed with some concern about the stress it was producing.

The stressors that arise within the work setting may be divided into the following broad categories:

1   The job content and/or the environment in which it is performed
2   The way the work is structured
3   Role in the organization
4   Interpersonal relations at work
5   Change

THE JOB CONTENT AND ENVIRONMENT

Much work has been done linking certain features of work tasks and working conditions with stress reactions. Exposures to toxic agents such as chemicals, fumes, dusts, and radiation can not only be physically stressful, but the mere concern that they might possibly reach dangerous levels in the workplace can also be a potent stressor. Intense noise, even if below the levels associated with hearing damage, is intrinsically stressful; it also makes communication difficult and inhibits social interaction among workers.

Inadequate lighting and glare are well-known stressors. I recall hearing of one instance in which the quality of the light produced a problem. It involved a group of women sitting at a long worktable assembling electronic devices in a large room brightly illuminated by long rows of unshielded fluorescent lamps. To allow visitors to view the process from the sumptuously decorated and dimly lit reception area of the adjacent executive offices, a large plate-glass window was installed in the wall that these workers faced. Almost immediately, there was an epidemic of illness with symptoms that baffled the plant physician and a rise in the number of faulty units that failed to pass inspection. Investigators finally traced the problem to the stress produced in the workers by the sight of their faces under the ghastly purplish light reflected by the mirrorlike plate glass of the new window. It was solved by increasing the light in the reception area and switching to rose-tinted fluorescent lamps to provide a softer light in the work area.

The layout of a factory unit is usually dictated by the work flow and the kinds of materials involved. Greater flexibility is possible in areas occupied by clerical and white-collar workers. I have been struck by what appears to be a fashion cycle, much like the length of women's skirts, alternating between large open areas and various kinds of partitioning. Both extremes can be stressful: Some individuals find it difficult to concentrate amid the sights and sounds of the open office, while others are troubled by the isolation and confinement of a small room, despite the status so often symbolized by a private office. Some organizations split the difference by girding the open work area with carrels or small cubicles to be used when employees desire some solitude.

The location of the work site may be important. For many, commuting to and from the workplace is much more stressful than the job itself. Those whose work entails frequent trips away from home must contend not only with such stressors of travel as fatigue, jet-lag, and strange surroundings, but also with separation from family and non-work activities.

Overload has deservedly received much attention as a stressor. It may be quantitative (having "too much to do") or qualitative ("too difficult"). Quantitative overload may be simply a matter of long hours without adequate rest periods, as with excessive overtime or moonlighting. The woman worker is frequently subjected to such overload when she has to perform all of her traditional housekeeping and child-care duties in her off hours. Overload can be created by too many phone calls, office visitors, meetings, and other work interruptions or by the imposition of unrealistic deadlines for the completion of difficult tasks.

Qualitative overload is experienced by air-traffic controllers, surgeons, television directors, and others whose work demands continuous concentration and rapid, meaningful decisions. It is also characteristic of individuals with a strong sense of responsibility for the quality of their work that is challenged by the requirement to speed up their activities. These include various kinds of craft workers, accountants and auditors (particularly at tax time), and the staffs of overcrowded hospital emergency rooms and intensive care units. At the Beth Israel Medical Center in New York City, a psychiatrist was assigned to conduct a program of group therapy and individual counseling for the staff of the Coronary Care Unit to help them cope with the combined stress of qualitative overload and disappointment over the failure of some patients to respond to their heroic efforts. It was prompted by the plaintive complaint of one of the nurses that she "had no time to cry."

There is good evidence that overload invariably leads to breakdown. It may be sudden and immediate as in "battle fatigue," or subtle and gradual, as in an increased incidence of heart attacks and premature deaths among a cohort of workers with similar exposures.

Underload can also cause difficulty. Boredom, lack of stimulation, the lack of opportunity to use acquired skills and abilities, and the repetitive performance of seemingly meaningless tasks are examples of underload. Dr. Clinton G. Weiman of Cornell University Medical College recently conducted a study of over 1,500 executives of a large financial organization in New York City who were voluntary participants in its periodic health examination program. The complete medical examination was supplemented by an inquiry that established the levels of job stress as perceived by the executives, and the results were correlated with the number of diseases or significant risk factors revealed by the examinations. As one might expect, those in the high-stress range had a significantly higher incidence of disease. Surprisingly, so did those in the opposite, low-stress end of the curve. They were somewhat fewer in number, a finding which Dr. Weiman infers might reflect the loss of some in this category by resignation from the organization (Weiman, 1977).

JOB STRUCTURE

Some jobs are structured so that the worker is simultaneously exposed to both overload and underload. The assembly line is the classic example. While it may not always be physically demanding, it involves constant attention and concentration, and there is unremitting time pressure. It presents, at the same time, the dehumanizing boredom of repetitive, highly standardized movements, monotony, a total absence of any intellectual involvement, and a lack of opportunity for social interaction and cooperation in the course of the work.

The regimentation and discipline imposed by assembly-line work are potent stressors. A frequently cited complaint is the need to get a supervisor's permission to leave a machine to go to the restroom. "Not everybody can wait," said a postal worker, "but if you've got to go to the washroom and you're not on a break, they say you're abusing washroom privileges."

The stressor effect of work on prolonged and especially on rotating shifts has generated much attention. The impact on biological rhythms is noted elsewhere (see pp. 132ff). Apart from this, the major difficulty created by shift work is its inhibition of full participation in family and social life. For those who rotate shifts, there is also the repeated stress of frequent adjustment to the new patterns. This was evidenced in a study of workers engaged in printing a large metropolitan newspaper among whom accidents were most frequent on the first day of the new shift.

ROLE IN THE ORGANIZATION

The individual's role at work is a significant source of stress. The pathfinding studies of Robert L. Kahn et al. (1964) at the University of Michigan's Institute for Social Research have generated much attention to what they labeled "role ambiguity" and "role conflict." Role ambiguity exists when an individual has insufficient information to perform his or her job. The individual is uncertain about the scope and responsibilities of the job, about the objectives it is supposed to achieve, and about coworkers' expectations of what will be accomplished. Channels for the utilization of skills and abilities are either unclear or ambiguous. The individual just doesn't know how he or she fits into the organization and is unsure of any rewards no matter how well he or she may perform.

Role conflict exists when the individual is torn by conflicting job demands, by differences of opinion with superiors, by having to do things he or she really doesn't want to do, or by difficulty in handling subordinates. The last difficulty also creates ambiguity when it is not clear how much authority an individual has over others.

A good example of role ambiguity and conflict is the management trainee in a large service organization who was directed by a senior vice president to survey the operation of a particular department. He was given a deadline for presenting his written report but no information about why the survey was being done other than the intimation that the department was not performing efficiently. At his first meeting with the department head, he learned that at least two similar surveys had been made in the recent past but the reports had never been released nor had they generated any apparent action. While his reception was cordial, it was made clear that he represented a burden, the department head expressing concern about the extent to which he would intrude on the time of subordinates. As he went around the department, it became quite clear that some of the people were "stone-walling" by being very slow to assemble the data he requested. Much of it, he found, was incomplete and some even inaccurate. He was not sure that he had sufficient authority to command their full cooperation although he suspected that, even with it, he would not get all the help he needed. He finished the survey and submitted the report on schedule but, other than a perfunctory note of thanks, was given no feedback. He did find out later that his recommendations had not been implemented but he was never told why.

Common sources of conflict in large organizations are office politics, territorial disputes over boundaries of responsibility, and competition for status symbols. These have been portrayed so frequently that examples would seem to be superfluous.

Other features of organizational life that cause stress are inequities in financial rewards, lack of promotional opportunities, and unreasonable or unfairly applied work rules. A very potent stressor for many is the absence of participation in decision making, especially when the decision relates to what the individual will be doing, how, and where.

INTERPERSONAL RELATIONS

As in the family and social life in the community, interpersonal relations are probably the most frequent source of stress in the work setting. It may arise in large, uncohesive work units or stem from isolation and lack of opportunities to interact with others. It can come from lack of acceptance by coworkers or feelings of being discriminated against by supervisors or the organization itself. Authoritarian bosses or likeable milksops unable to command any discipline can be equally stressful.

The inconsiderate boss or coworker who makes unreasonable demands can be troublesome. I once warned a company president to stop telephoning his European production manager whenever he wanted a bit of information. There was no crisis, and in fact, things were going quite well, in no small measure reflecting the skill and hard work of that manager. Due to the time differential, he was getting these calls at all hours, sometimes two or three times a night. Besides interrupting his sleep, they often seemed to question information he had reported earlier or to suggest that he might be making a mistake. The president persisted and the manager, who lacked assertiveness and was given to moments of self-doubt, wisely took the only course open to him: He resigned and joined a competing organization. It took six months for the president to hire a new production head whose performance never matched that of his predecessor. In the meantime, the manager, happily ensconced in his new organization, achieved new levels of success that made the organization a much more formidable competitor to the one he had left.

Sometimes, relationships with customers, clients, and other persons outside the organization are more troublesome than those with coworkers. Jobs dealing with the "public" are very stressful when the individual must curb righteous anger at the outrageous indignities to which he or she may be subjected. Police, prison guards, and other law-enforcement personnel are not only stressed by shift work, long hours, and monotony interspersed with episodes of extraordinary physical danger; they also have to contend with suspicion, prejudice, and outright hostility.

Airline-ticket agents must face the resentment of travelers holding tickets on overbooked flights and smilingly calm a horde of angry passengers with what may well be fictitious explanations for a repeatedly delayed plane departure. Workers staffing complaint departments need to develop "thick skins."

Sometimes, the difficulty stems from personal involvement in the problems of the people with whom the workers must deal. This is best illustrated by the need for professional emotional support for the staffs of hospices and other institutions caring for the terminally ill. The emotional investment required to be effective often makes the inevitable loss of the patient stressful enough to require professional assistance in dealing with grief.

CHANGE

Perhaps the most ubiquitous stressor encountered in the work setting is change. Obviously, it is much easier to adjust to change that is perceived as beneficial, but any change can be stressful. The threat of change and the expectation of it even after it has been announced are sometimes more stressful than the change itself.

We have already referred to the loss of job following a plant shutdown (see p. 18) and, later, will be discussing stress in relation to relocation (see p. 136). Company takeovers, mergers, and divestitures are changes involving total organizations that seem to be happening more frequently. Ranking with these in terms of the sweep of its effects is a change in chief executive officer. Even when planned as a normal succession rather than dictated by operational deficiencies, it frequently means a new management style and a "shake-up" in key executive positions that may have far-reaching, ripplelike effects.

The change may involve people: a new supervisor, the first entry of blacks, women, or "foreigners" into a work group, combining, splitting, or reconstituting work groups, etc. Or the change may involve moving to a new area in the plant, replacements for obsolete machinery and equipment, new materials, a new product, or simply a change in the work process. Although it may be embraced by some, it is often disconcerting to many. It is especially stressful to individuals who have a personal identification with the old or a lack of confidence in their capacity to adjust to the new.

Change is most stressful when it is imposed arbitrarily without permitting any involvement of those affected by it in decisions relating to its nature, extent, or timing and without full explanations of the reasons for it and what is expected to come of it.

THE VALUE OF STRESS

It must not be inferred that stress is inevitably harmful and undesirable. To hark back to Selye's concept of stress as the sum total of reactions to the multiplicity of internal and external stressors converging on the individual at any given moment, it can be useful and pleasurable. The challenges of a job, work that is structured to exercise acquired capabilities and develop new ones, a meaningful role in the organization, helpful and supportive relationship's with one's fellow workers, and change for the better: These suggest ways in which the stressors in the work setting can lead to satisfaction and well-being. Although it should be used with care, a stressor can be deliberately activated to have a therapeutic effect as in using the threat of job loss as a motivating factor in the treatment of alcoholism among workers (see p. 102).

REFERENCES

Cobb, S., and S. V. Kasl (1978). *Termination: The consequences of job loss.* Cincinnati: National Institute of Occupational Safety and Health, Division of Biomedical and Behavioral Science (Publication No. 76-1261).

Kahn, R. L.; D. M. Wolfe; R. P. Quinn; J. D. Snoek; and R. A. Rosenthal (1964). *Organizational Stress: Studies in Role Conflict and Ambiguity.* New York: Wiley.

Weiman, C. G. (Feb. 1977). A study of occupational stressors and the incidence of disease/risk. *J. Occupational Med.* 19:119-122.

PART II
STRESS-MANAGEMENT PROGRAMS

4

STRESS MANAGEMENT IN THE WORK SETTING

The fundamental goal of a stress-management program in the work setting is to reduce the burden of stress-related emotional and behavioral problems on individual employees and collectively on the work organization. It works to identify individuals experiencing difficulty and encourage them to seek the help they need. In fact, its very presence acts to legitimize their problems and remove from them the stigma associated with emotional difficulty which, although markedly diminished, is still all too prevalent. Its ready availability contrasts with the usual difficulty and delay in reaching appropriate sources of professional help in the community and the fact that, even when employees finally get an appointment, the staff is rarely familiar with the kinds of stressors workers commonly encounter. A major objective is the identification of particularly susceptible workers and anticipation of unusually stressful situations so that difficulty can be prevented.

WHO IS THE CLIENT?

The primary target is the individual employee. There are, however, two types of circumstances in which members of the employee's family may become involved:

1 In many instances, an employee's difficulty stems from a problem of his or her spouse or a dependent. When this problem is carried to

the workplace, its effect may be aggravated by the stressors of the job. The employee may be referred to resources in the community through which the problem can be approached more effectively. Except where the program provides services to employees' dependents, direct contact with the troubled family member is usually not made.

2   Direct contact with a family member may be made when understanding of the employee's difficulty might strengthen supportive attitudes and activities in the home that can enhance its resolution. This is particularly helpful in providing more accurate insight into the influence of work and the work situation on the employee's difficulty than he or she is able to offer. Occasionally, a union representative or co-worker can serve as a communicating link between the family and the workplace or, when there is no family, provide the social support that is often so helpful.

In some instances, the work unit may be the client. The fact that a number of its members may be experiencing difficulties at the same time suggests that there may be a common problem. The symptoms may be quite similar, as in mass psychogenic illness (see p. 116), but more often they are varied, reflecting the special susceptibilities of different individuals. In many cases, the problem may be traced to the disruptive effect of illness in the supervisor or a group leader. In fact, such a group reaction may lead to the detection of such a difficulty even before that individual is fully aware that he or she has it.

Often, however, the problem is attributable to a stressor to which the entire work unit has been subjected. The stressor may be real or only perceived; it may reflect toxic factors in the work processes or the environment, or changes in the status of that work group in the organization. A group approach involving meetings in which the problem is discussed and concerns are ventilated is usually indicated. Even when the factors creating the stressor cannot be eliminated, such an approach often succeeds in alleviating much of its adverse effect.

Sometimes, it is the organization as a whole that is in difficulty. Except for helping individual employees to cope more effectively, the stress-management program can do little to help when that difficulty reflects factors entirely beyond its control, such as depletion of essential resources, an economic downturn, or a declining industry. Even when the problem is remediable by changes in top management and management style, it is only rarely that the stress-management-program staff can capture the attention of persons strategically positioned in the organization to suggest appropriate action. It is much more likely that, under such circumstances, the organization will turn to outside consultants who may find the observations of the stress-management-program staff singularly helpful in framing their recommendations.

TYPES OF PROGRAMS

There is an almost infinite variety of stress-management programs reflecting the multiplicity of factors that influence their design and determine the scope of their activities. These include the perceived concerns of the organization and the needs of its employees, the availability of professional staff persons and the nature of their capabilities and interests, the extent of the resources the organization is willing to allocate for this purpose, and so on. A tragic episode involving the breakdown or death of a popular or highly placed individual or the sudden awareness of the impact on the organization of the difficulties of a cluster of individuals may not only stimulate the initiation of the program but frequently may determine the kind or kinds of problem at which it will be targeted.

It is not surprising, therefore, that stress-management programs operate under a variety of labels. Some indicate the specific problem on which they are focused: alcohol or drug abuse program, absence control program, etc. Others are more general: the Emotional Health Program at Equitable Life, the Employee Counseling Program at the 3M Company, the Employee Assistance Center at B. F. Goodrich, and Citibank's Staff Advisory Service. Illinois Bell has a Health Evaluation Program and Caterpillar Tractor offers Special Health Services, while I.B.M. and Gillette, using no special label, simply include these activities in their employee health programs. General Mills has both a Counseling Program and an Alcoholism Program, and J. C. Penney, emphasizing the role of managers and supervisors in case finding, recently initiated a Job Performance Action Program aimed primarily at alcohol and drug abuse.

Originally, labels such as Mental Hygiene or Mental Health Program were used. To get away from the connotation of serious psychiatric disease, companies began to refer to them as Emotional Health Programs. A further step was taken in December 1978, when the Washington Business Group on Health and the Boston University Center for Industry and Health Care jointly sponsored a conference on Employee Mental Wellness Programs. Currently, Troubled Employee Programs and Employee Assistance Programs seem to be the most popular labels, but as the role of stress is receiving greater recognition, the term Stress-Management Program is becoming more widely used.

The point is that the label does not always indicate the nature of the program. In one organization, for example, an Employee Assistance Program deals only with alcohol abuse while in another using the same label, the program addresses a broad sweep of employee problems ranging from frank mental illness to car-pool arrangements. Some organizations retain the same label as the scope of the program broadens while others change the name to enhance its acceptability or merely to "keep up with the Joneses." Thus we should be cautious in comparing programs and look beyond the label to identify its objectives and the activities it undertakes.

Stress-management programs also vary widely in the way they are staffed and the place in organizational structure they occupy. Staffing ranges from the part-time assignment of a layperson with some training in counseling to a group of multidisciplinary professionals supported by administrative and clerical personnel. At Equitable Life, the program is part of the Employee Health Services Department, while across town, at Metropolitan Life, it functions under the Personnel Department. At General Mills in Minneapolis, it is provided outside the organization through contracts with two independent, private clinics whose activities are coordinated by Corporate Medical Director James Craig.

Despite such variability, it is possible to divide stress-management programs into two prototypes: a clinical or medical model and an organizational model or approach. The former deals on a one-to-one basis with individuals and their problems. The latter deals with units or segments of the work force or the employee population as a whole and with the problems of the organization as a functional entity. Two major distinctions between these and their analogues in the community are their emphasis on work performance and functional effectiveness as an index of well-being and the attention given to preventive activities.

The clinical program

Although the clinical model is based on the traditional medical approach to treatment, it is sometimes used to address such non-medical problems as financial difficulties, job placement, and career counseling. It focuses on one person at a time and comprises the following elements:

1   *First Aid*—Providing immediate contact with a professional either in person or by telephone. To a person suffering from acute anxiety, the mere reassurance that help is available may defuse a crisis that might otherwise precipitate a bout of decompensation. For the most part, it involves referring the individual to a source of help in the community appropriate to his or her problem.

2   *Case Finding*—Identifying persons with indications of a stress-related difficulty and making arrangements for its evaluation. In most instances, individuals who have recognized that they are having difficulty present themselves for help. Often they are identified when the staff of an employee health unit alertly notes a pattern of somatic complaints that may have an emotional origin. Many organizations have established procedures through which supervisors refer for evaluation employees with increased absenteeism or failing work performance, or whose appearance or behavior seems unusual, especially when this represents a change.

3   *Evaluation*—Establishing an appropriate diagnosis and estimating the severity and the tempo of the difficulty. It includes the identification of significant precipitating or aggravating factors and a determination of whether the individual is able—or should be allowed—to continue on the job.

4   *Treatment*—Providing short-term counseling and supportive therapy in the workplace. Almost without exception, individuals requiring prolonged or definitive therapy are referred to health professionals or facilities in the community. It would take very few such cases to preempt all of the available staff time and energy and bring all of the other elements of the program virtually to a standstill. Further, since the availability of the program is usually restricted to active employees, the therapeutic relationship which is so important to the success of treatment would have to be disrupted if the individual left or had to be separated from the organization before its goals were reached.

5   *Referral*—Making arrangements for the individual to receive the treatment most suited to his or her needs. This requires a knowledge of the availability, capability, quality, and cost of private practitioners, clinics, hospitals, specialized facilities, and programs in the community. These must be matched against the individual's needs and tolerances in terms of urgency, convenience, pocketbook, and prejudices. For example, treatment would not be successful if it imposed a financial burden beyond the individual's means or if it required asso-

ciation with groups or backgrounds (e.g., age, religion, ethnic origin, etc.) in which he or she would be uncomfortable. Of particular importance to the individual attempting to continue to work while in therapy is the availability of an appointment schedule that will not seriously compromise job attendance.

Successful referral involves more than telling the individual where to go. It requires preparation for the intake procedures imposed by the treating facility so that he or she will not be overwhelmed by bureaucratic inquiries, paperwork, and delays. More important, it requires explanations of what to expect and reassurance that alternatives are available if the proposed arrangement proves to be entirely unworkable. All this may require several sessions with the individual; in fact, it probably should be labeled "preparation for therapy." Finally, it should involve a follow-up to verify that the individual did not "drop out" but has actually embarked on treatment.

6 *Rehabilitation*—Facilitating continuation on the job during therapy and/or return to work after a bout of disability. For the individual who continues on the job, this involves adjustments of work schedules and assignments that will accommodate the treatment schedule and minimize stressful responsibilities, tasks, and interpersonal relationships that might impede recovery. A frequently important consideration is the reassignment of employees for whom drugs are prescribed that might impair alertness and reaction time and lead to accidents (e.g., fire fighters, aircraft crews, vehicle operators, and those working with fast-moving and hazardous machinery). For the individual whose illness dictates absence from work, it involves observing to make sure that he or she is making satisfactory progress and keeping the supervisor informed of the individual's expected return so that arrangements can be made to cover his or her assigned responsibilities while away. Depending on the severity and duration of illness, the employee's return may require a period of readjustment to work or, in some instances, retraining for a totally new assignment.

7 *Screening*—Periodic examination of individuals in highly stressful positions to detect early indications of impending difficulty or the routine evaluation of employee groups to identify those with characteristics that make them particularly susceptible to difficulty.

8 *Prevention*—Educating and persuading individuals at high risk for difficulty either because of their personal characteristics or the nature of their work to adopt life-styles and work habits that will

enhance their capacities to cope and to adapt. It also involves following individuals with a prior history of difficulty to be sure that precautions aimed at preventing recurrences are being observed.

While clinical programs in the work setting have much in common with those provided by practitioners and facilities in the community, there are important advantages that make them especially valuable to the work organization. These include:

1 Ready availability and ease of access.

2 Focus on short-term counseling and resolution of crises for individuals who might not be regarded as sick enough to justify appropriate attention by therapeutic resources in the community.

3 Knowledge of and opportunity to modify job-related factors that can aggravate an individual's difficulty or impede its resolution.

4 Emphasis on effective referral as described above rather than "disposition."

5 Emphasis on the preservation of work capacity and its prompt restoration after bouts of difficulty.

6 Opportunity to follow and reach out to individuals who may resist recognition of the nature of their difficulties or acceptance of the help needed to handle them more effectively.

7 Emphasis on the prevention of difficulty and its early recognition when prevention fails.

Needless to say, these advantages will be realized only when the program in the work setting is properly designed, placed, and staffed and is operated in a way that earns the respect and trust of those it is intended to serve.

The organizational program

Organizational programs are aimed more broadly at an entire employee population. They are sometimes extensions of the clinical program and are run as a staff function. More often, however, they function independently under the direction of the person responsible for personnel relations or a manager responsible for operations. Although their continuing operation usually resides within the organization, they are frequently designed and monitored by consultants retained for this purpose. More often than not, they are stimulated by reports of high levels of employee discontent and difficulty, by acute crises or disruptions of labor-management relations, or by significant impending organizational changes such as automation of a process, relocation of a plant, or production of a new line of products or services. Sometimes, they reflect the concern of a new management about matters to which its predecessor had become inured or had taken for granted, or they represent a response to the demands of a union.

Fundamentally, these programs address the policies and practices of the organization as they relate to job stress and the emotional climate of the workplace. They include the establishment of criteria for hiring and placement, mechanisms for disciplining unsatisfactory behavior and performance, training in leadership and supervision, and devices for effective communication with and between all levels of the work force. In many instances, they reflect the results of attitude surveys that probe for the sources of employees' concerns and dissatisfaction. In recent years, such programs have also addressed the disruption of group units by the perceived injustices and other problems created by affirmative-action programs for the hiring and advancement of minorities, women, and the handicapped.

Some organizational programs are more closely related to the clinical program. These are designed to create greater awareness and understanding of stress-related problems and to remove the stigma attached to them when they produce emotional and behavioral disorders. Educational activities focus on such common problems as alcoholism, drug abuse, aging, and marital difficulties. Informational activities encourage utilization of the in-house clinical program or its counterparts outside the organization and promote support of worthwhile programs and facilities in the community.

Some organizational programs, however, focus on the organization itself as a functional entity and address such problems as clarifying goals and objectives, management style, and internal communications. These are discussed in more detail in Chapter 7.

The preventive program

It has long been recognized that the work setting is a particularly propitious location for activities aimed at the elimination or control of stressors. They benefit not only the organization and its employees, but also their families and the community at large. They permeate the clinical and organizational programs and include the following major elements:

1   Establishment of work practices and an emotional climate throughout the organization that will enhance human well-being and performance.

2   Education and motivation of employees to maintain healthier work habits and personal life-styles.

3   Provision of special programs to assist employees, especially those identified as being "high risk," to deal more effectively with stress and obviate its potentially harmful effects.

4   Identification and appropriate modification of high-risk jobs and work situations.

Some of these are dictated by today's concepts of the organization's legal and moral responsibility for the health and well-being of its personnel. Others are justified by the ease and economy of reaching a "captive audience" and the enhanced effectiveness afforded by the influence of the organization and the peer pressures within the work group.

CONFIDENTIALITY AND PRIVACY

The confidentiality of all personal information acquired in the course of any program for dealing with work-related stress must be strictly and scrupulously maintained. This categorical statement can be justified on the basis of a host of ethical, moral, and legal considerations. Overriding all of them, however, is the pragmatic reality that the program will not succeed if confidentiality is breached. Stated simply, if the employees lack confidence in the integrity of the program staff and are concerned that the information about them that is assembled might be divulged in a way that could embarrass them or affect their job status and security, they will be uncooperative and will dissemble or conceal any difficulty they may be experiencing.

I have uncovered many instances in which employees elected not to apply for health insurance benefits to which they were unquestionably entitled because the claim forms on which the diagnosis and nature of treatment had to be entered were filed through the personnel department. There is no way this can be avoided in an organization that is self-insured and administers all claims internally. When a carrier processes the claims, it is customary for the completed form to be reviewed first by the personnel department to verify the claimant's eligibility for the benefits. This is important not only to establish that he or she is a current member of the insured group but, in large organizations with a number of different insurance programs, to indicate the extent of the coverage.

Special arrangements can be made when there may be some sensitivity, but the very need to apply for them defeats the employee's desire for anonymity. This can be obviated by simply modifying the procedure so that the eligibility of the claim is verified first, before it goes to the physician or other health-care provider. After the sensitive information is entered, the form is forwarded directly to the carrier for payment. Most carriers train their claims personnel to respect the confidentiality of the information they handle, but this is usually superfluous. They handle so many claims, usually from people from a number of organizations in dispersed geographic locations, that unless the claimant happens to be a very prominent public figure, there is virtually no likelihood of anyone taking a personal interest in the nature of the problem.

Even this level of anonymity can be defeated when the carrier provides the organization with a periodic summary of its claims experience. In many instances, this is supplied in the form of a computer printout of a list of paid claims in which the individual claimants are identified by name and location and the diagnosis is given. This is easily remedied by requesting the carrier to block out the columns identifying individual claimants and supply only the summary data.

The point of all this is that there must be assurance that mechanisms are in place to limit the use of personal information to those who must have it for acceptable purposes and to guard against even inadvertent release to others. This extends to such questions as where the files are located and who has access to them. In organizations where records are kept on computer tape, there must be evidence of satisfactory security procedures.

Company files have traditionally been labeled "confidential," but that label has generally been applied to restrict the employee, not the management. Management has considered it appropriate to collect personal information about the worker that includes not only performance appraisals, comments volunteered by supervisors, and records of attendance and any disciplinary actions, but also medical information and communications about the worker's financial status and personal life. Workers are rightfully concerned about the use of such information as a basis for promotion, demotion, or discharge, especially when much of the information not only may lack relevance, but may actually be incorrect. Workers are also concerned about the release of that information to others without their knowledge, much less their consent. These concerns, part of the general concern about the privacy of personal information held by government agencies and private organizations, have been sparked by evidence of carelessness and abuse. Laws have been enacted that establish policies for federal and state agencies, and many organizations in the private sector have voluntarily adopted similar policies hoping to forestall more stringent and needlessly costly governmental regulations (Gorlin, 1977). Medical organizations, notably the American Occupational Medical Association, have published policies and position papers to guide their members in dealing with this problem. The Code of Ethics of that organization has several items that deal with confidentiality (see Table 4.1).

As pointed out in a symposium on the "Confidentiality of Occupational Health Records" at the American Occupational Health Conference held in Cincinnati in April 1976, many of the governmental policies and regulations are in conflict (Warshaw, 1976). Dealing with the sensitive issue of confidentiality, therefore, requires devotion to established ethical principles, a strong sense of equity and fairness, objectivity, and common sense.

In every stress-management program the staff will become privy to a great deal of information about individuals' personal lives as well as their jobs and their relationships at work. The commitment to its confidentiality can create some very contentious situations and troublesome issues for which there may be no clearcut solution. One such issue, the question of limits to confidentiality, is illustrated by the following cases:

1   An employee told his wife that he was receiving counseling for the relief of symptoms that he attributed to a work-related problem. To the counselor, he revealed that their real source was some difficulty with an extramarital romance. When the wife called the counselor to indicate her concern at the impact of the husband's symptoms on her and their children, expressed her concern at their slowness in receding, and demanded to know "what the employer was doing about the job problem" and what she could do to help, how should the counselor have responded?

2   If the employee confesses to falsifying records or producing faulty work, does the counselor report this to management?

TABLE 4.1 *Code of ethical conduct for physicians providing occupational medical services.* *

These principles are intended to aid physicians in maintaining ethical conduct in providing occupational medical service. They are standards to guide physicians in their relationships with the individuals they serve, with employers and workers' representatives, with colleagues in the health professions, and with the public.

Physicians should:
1. accord highest priority to the health and safety of the individual in the workplace;
2. practice on a scientific basis with objectivity and integrity;
3. make or endorse only statements which reflect their observations or honest opinion;
4. actively oppose and strive to correct unethical conduct in relation to occupational health service;
5. avoid allowing their medical judgment to be influenced by any conflict of interest;
6. strive conscientiously to become familiar with the medical fitness requirements, the environment and the hazards of the work done by those they serve, and with the health and safety aspects of the products and operations involved;
7. treat as confidential whatever is learned about individuals served, releasing information only when required by law or by overriding public health considerations, or to other physicians at the request of the individual according to traditional medical ethical practice; and should recognize that employers are entitled to counsel about the medical fitness of individuals in relation to work, but are not entitled to diagnoses or details of a specific nature;
8. strive continually to improve medical knowledge, and should communicate information about health hazards in timely and effective fashion to individuals or groups potentially affected, and make appropriate reports to the scientific community;
9. communicate understandably to those they serve any significant observations about their health, recommending further study, counsel, or treatment when indicated;
10. seek consultation concerning the individual or the workplace whenever indicated;
11. cooperate with governmental health personnel and agencies, and foster and maintain sound ethical relationships with other members of the health professions; and
12. avoid solicitation of the use of their services by making claims, offering testimonials, or implying results which may not be achieved, but they may appropriately advise colleagues and others of services available.

* Adopted by the Board of Directors of the American Occupational Medical Association, July 23, 1976

3   What does the counselor tell management when an employee refuses to turn down an important overseas assignment even though that employee has personal or family problems that will probably lead to failure in the assignment at a considerable cost to the organization?

4   What actions does the counselor take when a paranoid employee relates plans to sabotage expensive machinery or to do bodily harm to the supervisor?

Except for the last case, in which court decisions have established that counselors are required to warn intended victims of their potential danger and to take any actions required to protect them, counselors must remain silent. They should make every effort to persuade the employee to confess the damaging information or allow the counselor to divulge it but, if the employee insists, the counselor must remain mute. By design, counselors serve as the agents of the employee even against the immediate interests of the organization. This must be explicitly stated in the written policy that guides the stress-management program.

Another frequently difficult question concerns the amount of information that may be divulged to a supervisor who has referred an employee because of obvious difficulty. A related question is what information managers can expect to receive that will help them facilitate the rehabilitation and reentry of a decompensated employee. The proper answer is no more than the employee wishes to have divulged. A simple statement that the employee is or is not capable of working at the job without concern for his or her safety and the well-being of others may be made, but a diagnostic label and details of the problem may not be revealed without the employee's express consent.

Except in rare instances, I have had no difficulty persuading employees that information that could affect their work status or future careers should be made available to their supervisor or an appropriate person in management. Whenever possible, I arranged for the employee to sit in on the discussion or to read the written report so that he or she knew exactly what was being said.

Oddly enough, I have usually found that the nature of the employee's difficulty is well known throughout the organization, thanks to the employee having revealed it to one or more coworkers who fed it into the organization's "grapevine," that miracle of ancient communication. In fact, a persuasive argument for allowing me to discuss it with the supervisor is the desirability of deflating some of the exaggerations often embodied in the rumors. Nevertheless, even if it is generally known, one's refusal to allow its revelation must be respected and every precaution taken to make sure that the professionals staffing the stress-management program cannot be accused of leaking it.

Managers often manifest a desire for information about a particular employee's problems. This may reflect a sincere desire to be helpful, an attempt to manipulate the employee's job status so that he or she is less troublesome to the organization, or simple curiosity. For this reason, an explicit policy calling for confidentiality is a vital ingredient to the success of the stress-management program and the continuing reeducation of managers on all levels with respect to the importance of heeding it is an essential activity of its staff.

A corollary issue is the matter of the employees' access to their own records. Although many organizations would resist allowing employees to inspect and copy from the actual record, there is general agreement that they have a right to all of the information about them that it contains (under certain circumstances, it may be advisable not to reveal the sources of specific items of information—but these should be rare). I would go even further: I regard it as a professional obligation to see not only that they are given the information, but that every effort is made to be sure that they understand it and appreciate its implications. Further, they should have the opportunity to note any disagreement with it in the record.

As this is written, the issues that surround confidentiality and privacy are still in flux. Laws dealing with health-related records are being promoted by anecdotes and "horror stories" in which these principles were abused. As pointed out in the Cincinnati symposium, the problem lies not so much in the content of the information but in the way it is interpreted and used. In over thirty years as an occupational physician and consultant, thanks to slavish adherence to the ethical principles and practices described above, the companion issues of confidentiality and privacy have presented no difficulty either to me or to the organizations with which I have been affiliated.

REFERENCES

Gorlin, H. (Sept. 1977). *Privacy in the Workplace.* New York, The Conference Board, Information Bulletin No. 27.

Warshaw, L. J. (Aug. 1976). Confidentiality versus the need to know. *J. Occup. Med.* **18**:534–536.

5

KINDS OF HELPERS

Persons seeking professional help with stress-induced difficulty or outright emotional illness, whether for themselves or for people in their organization, face the knotty problem of selecting the right kinds of "helpers." They soon discover that there are many different kinds of practitioners with more or less formal training and with all sorts of credentials or none at all. While some are generalists, others specialize in one brand of therapy, often offering it with evangelistic ardor as *the* way to health while denigrating the treatments offered by others. By one recent count there were some 130 different systems or schools of psychotherapy.

In ordinary medical illness, it's comparatively easy. One either goes to a general practitioner, family practitioner, or primary physician (individuals use different labels, but they all mean the same thing), or directly seeks out a specialist trained to deal with the particular organ or system involved. Thus, one is referred to a cardiologist for heart pain, to an endocrinologist for a sluggish thyroid, or an orthopedist for a deranged lumbar disc. Unless the original diagnosis was wrong—the "heart pain" could be an inflamed gall-bladder, the "sluggish thyroid" a mental depression, and the "deranged disc" a kidney stone—this usually works quite well. At least, the patient is in the right department of the "emporium" offering cures for all sorts of ailments.

It doesn't work the same way for emotional and mental illness, for behavioral disorders and stress-related difficulties. This "emporium" also has many departments staffed by professionals with different kinds of expertise who offer what appear to be vastly differing kinds of treatment, but they all treat the same kinds of problems. How is the layperson to select the one that best meets his or her needs?

To carry the analogy further, it reminds me of one of the aisles in a large department store formed by the side-by-side counters where individual cosmetic manufacturers offer their lines of beauty aids. The products are similar: perfumes, lotions, creams, paints, and polishes. They form a stunning mélange of provocative scents and dazzling containers, and each is offered with the strongest assurance that the particular brand will accomplish the desired miracle.

How is the consumer to decide? By the uniqueness of the packaging? By the attractiveness and persuasiveness of the salesperson? By price—is the least expensive the most economical or is the most costly a better buy because of the "more expensive" ingredients it contains? By apparent popularity—the one most advertised or enjoying the largest sales volume? By the prominence and beauty of those who provide testimonials of what it has done for them?

The truth is that most of the time, it doesn't matter which one is selected. To be sure, there are instances in which a particular product may prove irritating or, when the consumer is uniquely sensitive to one or more of its ingredients, it may even cause a devastating reaction. More rarely, there are cases in which a product successfully hides a "blemish" that eventually turns out to be a skin cancer or some other lesion for which definitive treatment may be less effective because of the delay. But most of the time, the product does do something for the purchaser. And even when it doesn't, the *feeling* that it does may alter the purchaser's attitudes and behavior so that the desired result may be achieved.

So it is in the treatment of emotional and behavioral problems. There is an ever-enlarging variety of professional and "semi- professional" therapists—among which there are inevitably a few charlatans and outright frauds—offering a constantly growing catalog of kinds of treatment. A few are truly innovative, being based on new discoveries or highly original theoretical formulations derived from accumulated experience. Most are improvements—or at least variations—of treatments with already demonstrated efficacy. And many are just-established treatments repackaged with a new "brand" name or provided in a different setting or format.

All too frequently, the basis of the consumer's choice is the same here as with the beauty aids: availability, price, the personality and persuasiveness of the therapist, popularity, testimonials, etc. And the results are also the same. Some individuals whose personalities cannot tolerate a particular treatment or who are unusually sensitive to one or more of its elements will be made worse, sometimes precipitously and devastatingly. Some may show an initial improvement that hides a much more serious underlying problem that may be much more difficult to treat when it finally emerges in full-blown form. Most, however, are helped and show varying degrees of improvement, sometimes short-lived but often long lasting. And many who are not really helped by the treatment show gratifying improvement: These we call the "placebo reactors."*

Sometimes the "fit" between the patient and the therapist contributes more than the kind of treatment employed. Similarly, the

---

* A placebo is a completely inactive, inert, and utterly useless medication or treatment—it has also been called a "sham" or "dummy" treatment—that is administered to delude the patient into thinking that he or she is receiving effective therapy. It is used most often as a tool in research to evaluate the utility of a new therapeutic agent or one of questionable efficacy. When the study is properly conducted and analyzed, a truly effective treatment will yield a significantly higher proportion of good results than the placebo. If it does not, it may be concluded that it is worthless, at least for that particular condition in the particular kind of population in which the study was performed.

Astonishingly, in countless studies of the treatment of virtually every kind of human disease conducted by hundreds of investigators since the 1940s when the placebo emerged as a valuable research instrument, it has consistently produced the desired results in about one-third of the cases. The benefits of the popular nostrums and many of the bestselling over-the-counter medicines have been shown to be due, not to their ingredients, but to the placebo effect. This is why one can place little credence in testimonials of the efficacy of a particular treatment; more often than not, they represent the placebo effect, the classical fallacy of *post hoc, ergo propter hoc* (after it, therefore because of it).

Repeated studies have failed to identify any consistent pattern of attributes or attitudes that distinguish the placebo reactor from individuals who do not respond. They also disprove the erroneous assumption that a response to the placebo brands the individual as "neurotic" or proves that his or her symptoms are feigned or imaginary. This must be emphasized: The placebo is similarly effective in all kinds of people with all kinds of organic as well as psychophysiological disorders. In fact, the only type of person in whom the placebo is rarely effective is the true malingerer.

This has significance in evaluating the effectiveness of solutions to human problems within the work organization. The benefits attributed to a particular intervention may represent the placebo effect or, as it is known to behavioral scientists, the "Hawthorne effect" (see p. 177), or they may reflect either a purely random fluctuation or the action of something entirely coincidental.

absence of a good patient-therapist relationship can block the effectiveness of the most consistently useful form of treatment. Even the placebo is more effective when such a relationship is present.

This is an important point. Even the most accomplished therapist will have some failures and the worst, some successes. Lack of a good "fit" should be discernible very early in the course of treatment and, rather than condemn the treatment as a failure, the individual should be referred to another practitioner. Successful referral requires knowledge of the personal characteristics of both the patient and the therapist so that a proper "fit" can be anticipated while the patient is prepared for the possibility that it just might not work out and he or she might have to try someone else.

The primary concern with the selection of a health professional to work within the organization or as a referral resource to whom employees may be sent is the appropriateness and quality of the services he or she provides. An important secondary consideration is the potential of claims of negligence against the organization as well as those individuals within it who were involved. It has been remarked that we are becoming an increasingly litigious society, and statistics demonstrate that successful claims are increasing both in number and the size of the awards they bring. Even unsuccessful claims are costly; they are disturbing, distracting, and their defense requires the use of expensive legal talent.

In many jurisdictions, the "fellow-servant doctrine" reduces the financial risk. The claims still have to be defended, but this doctrine, deeply entrenched in common law, prohibits an employee from bringing a tort action for negligence against a fellow worker or the employer. The employee's only recourse is a worker compensation claim, even though the condition for which he or she was treated or referred was totally unrelated to the work or the workplace. Although they are sometimes sizable, the awards in worker compensation cases are much smaller than those earned by successful negligence actions. (See p. 193ff for a discussion of worker compensation problems).

The fellow-servant doctrine is being eroded, however (Warshaw, 1977). Tort actions for negligence are increasingly being allowed across the country and, in several recent instances, plaintiffs' attorneys have celebrated a successful worker compensation claim by filing a second tort action for negligence based on essentially the same circumstances.

It should be noted that negligence cannot be claimed merely because the treatment or the referral did not help the patient, or even when it made the patient worse. A successful negligence action requires evidence that the organization was negligent in verifying the capabilities and qualifications of the therapist it employed or the practitioner to whom the organization or one of its staff referred the individual. This dictates that the organization be painstakingly circumspect in verifying the credentials and qualifications of all health professionals before they are hired and requiring that employees needing treatment be referred only to practitioners and facilities with proper accreditation and good reputations and only for treatments that have been recognized and generally accepted as appropriate to the circumstances of the particular case.

Now, having made the point that people with stress-related problems may be helped by a variety of professional personnel, it may be helpful to identify the categories more frequently involved with those problems arising in the work setting.

"POOR PEOPLE'S PSYCHIATRISTS"

These are the people in the community whose work generally includes listening to their customers' troubles: barbers, beauticians, bartenders, pharmacists, and small shopkeepers. Eugene Gauron, professor of psychiatry at the University of Iowa, studied how they work in small Iowa towns, and characterized them as being interested in people and possessing "the ability to listen with sympathetic gestures and mannerisms, leading the speakers to feel that they have found someone who understands their plight." By simply allowing people to ventilate their problems in a sympathetic, essentially nonjudgmental environment, they help to ease the stress the problems produce. When they go further, as many do, to sharpen the focus on the more important aspects of the problem and suggest that there may be other ways of looking at it, they are being therapeutic. Professor Gauron found that they often become a "kind of middleman for those with serious problems" by facilitating their acceptance of professional help.

Of course, it can work the other way. Many people have had the experience of being "trapped" in the chair while a barber or a beautician almost cheerfully regaled them with the saga of their own troubles. I recall a dentist who filled his patients' mouths with gauze pads and gadgets so that they could respond only with grunts and moans and, while he worked away at their teeth, he told them all about the difficulties he and his family were experiencing.

THE "UNOFFICIAL NETWORK"

Scattered through the rank and file of every organization is an unofficial network of individuals to whom employees turn when they need advice and help. These are not necessarily the designated leaders— e.g., foreman, supervisor, or union steward—or those with the greatest length of service. They are never the rabble-rousers, the busybodies, or the self-proclaimed authorities. They are simply people who have learned to listen sympathetically without being too judgmental, who do not gossip or carry tales, and whose advice has generally been found to be helpful without being overtly self-serving. They are generally quiet, unassuming people who, somehow, always find time for a fellow employee. They wear no badges and carry no titles, but it takes very little effort to find out who they are.

They constitute a valuable resource that can serve as a foundation on which to build an effective stress-management program. Any approach to these people, however, should be made informally with great delicacy and sensitivity. Thrusting them into the spotlight can not only destroy their usefulness but might be disruptive by being perceived as favoritism or an attempt to undermine the authority of appointed leaders.

The staff of the in-house program should identify these individuals and contrive to become acquainted with them.* As these individuals learn to understand the functions and the capabilities of the staff and appreciate its integrity and the sincerity of its interest, they will promote its utilization by the employees by referring some of their "clients" to it.

One note of caution: While many of these "helpers" are strong, healthy individuals who have successfully weathered their own emotional storms, some may be unconsciously using these relationships to satisfy their own psychic needs. For example, the senior secretary who becomes a kind of "house-mother" to a bevy of young clerks may be requiting the loss of a child or compensating for the fact that she can never have one. It requires considerable skill and subtlety to identify such situations and correct them without precipitating decompensa-

---

* This underscores the dictum that a program will not succeed if the staff simply sits in its office waiting for employees to appear or imperiously commands their presence. They must make frequent tours of the workplace to observe the nature and tempo of the work, to chat with employees, and to sense the emotional climate.

tion in these individuals and disrupting what may have been important social supports for those who have relied on them.

UNION COUNSELORS

Union stewards, shop-chairpersons, and in some locations, officially designated union counselors are frequently consulted by employees with difficulties attributed to the stressors of their work. Some, eager to make a mark as militant unionists, lose no opportunity to convert these difficulties into demands or formal grievances. Most of the time, however, unless there is already a climate of labor-management contentiousness, they reserve such actions for instances in which they are unquestionably necessary. Instead, they explore the nature of the problem with the employee. Being thoroughly familiar with what goes on in the workplace and, as a rule, directly or indirectly aware of personal difficulties that may be burdening the employee, they are frequently able to sort out those that originate in the workplace from those that are brought to it. They frequently provide sound advice, including referral for professional treatment to the union program if it has one, to the organization's in-house program if it has earned their respect and confidence, or to a community facility. When workplace factors cause or aggravate the problem, they are frequently able to persuade management to rectify them or to initiate special arrangements that will ease their impact on the employee until he or she has recovered the ability to tolerate them.

Union representatives are strategically placed and often quite skillful in mediating conflicts between two workers that otherwise might lead to a virtual "civil war" in the work group.

Despite their usual lack of formal education and training, it is heartwarming to note how seriously such union counselors take these responsibilities and how well they discharge them. To assist them, a number of unions have instituted special training programs to enhance their effectiveness and have arranged for the availability of high-ranking professionals to advise them in the handling of problem cases when the need arises.

Their value has been recognized by many managers. With the development of mutual respect, trust, and awareness of shared concerns, the badges of their traditional adversarial relationship are set aside as they join forces to help the troubled employee. This kind of collaboration requires acute sensitivity on the parts of both the union counselor and the manager to the need to avoid any action that might be perceived as subverting their formal responsibilities.

INDUSTRIAL CHAPLAINS AND PASTORAL COUNSELORS

Pastoral counselors or chaplains are members of the clergy who have supplemented their religious experience with special training in counseling. Many function in hospitals where they bring understanding and comfort to patients who need help in coping with the stresses imposed by their medical problems. A number—estimated to fall between 50 and 100—have taken full-time employment in industry, and many more serve as employee counselors on a part-time basis.

Some industrial chaplaincies are filled on a volunteer basis by either clergy and laypeople. The Institute of Industrial and Commercial Ministers, which deals only with such part-time, nonpaying chaplaincies, reports that about two dozen companies are currently using such services; they include Anheuser-Busch and Virginia Electric and Power.

Industrial chaplaincies originated in the Deep South but now have spread to all parts of the country. Most of the organizations that provide them are small to medium in size, although chaplains' offices are maintained by R. J. Reynolds (since 1949), Holiday Inns of America, and the Washington Group, Inc., a conglomerate whose 5,000 employees work in its seventeen textile mills and sixty food stores and ice cream shops. They seem to flourish in an atmosphere that is already religious and sometimes represent extensions of church activity into the plant. Thus, the Southern Baptist Convention's Home Mission Board in Atlanta has a Business and Industrial Chaplaincy section. Although the chaplains are usually identified with a particular religious group—they are maintained by most of the major churches—they are generally more interested in counseling employees than in proselytizing among them. Accordingly, they are often consulted by employees affiliated with different churches or none at all.

Most of the industrial chaplains deal only with the problems of individual employees. However, in New York City, Rabbi Seymour Siegel, Professor of Ethics at the Jewish Theological Seminary, meets regularly to discuss ethical and moral matters with the top management of Ruder and Finn, the large, well-known public relations firm.

There is some carping, based on the fact that most of the organizations with chaplains are not unionized and the suspicion that the chaplaincy represents a management ploy to cool any employee unrest that might lead to interest in union membership. And there is the inevitable suspicion that the industrial chaplain is being used as a "management spy." Nevertheless, they are flourishing, and interest among organizations in industrial chaplaincies seems to be growing.

HOLISTIC MEDICAL CLINICS

Holistic medicine is a relatively new movement that is just beginning to develop a particular interest in work-related problems. Because it provides highly effective care, especially in the management of disorders associated with stress, and does so with impressive cost savings compared to facilities offering traditional health care, organizations are beginning to refer troubled employees to the clinics where it is practiced (Pelletier, 1977).

These clinics are usually located in churches and staffed by a member of the clergy with some experience in pastoral counseling, a nurse practitioner, a social worker, and a part-time physician. New patients are seen by the paraprofessional team and are referred to the physician for diagnosis and treatment only when dictated by the nature or the apparent seriousness of the medical problem.

According to holistic medicine, all states of health and disease are psychosomatic, at least to some degree, and successful treatment requires attention to the mind and the spirit as well as to the body. It stipulates that both patient and therapist must share responsibility for the healing process. Illness provides an opportunity for patients to learn about themselves and to grow, but this will happen only when the healers know themselves and participate in the treatment as human beings rather than just as technologists.

The theoretical formulation of holistic medicine has not yet crystallized and it is expressed in varying forms by different practitioners. It has many detractors who look upon it as a partial retreat from "scientific" medicine back to faith healing. It is fortunate that its fees are usually very modest, since they are not always accepted for reimbursement by Blue Cross/Blue Shield and other health-insurance carriers. Nevertheless, it has demonstrated its ability to help people cope with stress-related problems and seems to be gaining adherents, especially among those who have been disenchanted by the impersonal, dehumanizing, assembly-line medical technology that is all too prevalent.

OCCUPATIONAL PHYSICIANS AND NURSES

The roles of these occupational-health professionals have been described elsewhere in this book; see pp. 64ff for occupational nurses and pp. 68ff for occupational physicians.

PSYCHIATRISTS

The psychiatrist is a physician who, following graduation from medical school, some general residency training, and often some experience in practice, spends another three to five years studying the theories and the diagnosis and treatment of mental and behavioral disorders in order to qualify for the examination leading to certification as a specialist in psychiatry. Most psychiatrists are members of the American Psychiatric Association, which will provide information about the background of any member on request. Committees and task forces of the American Psychiatric Association have addressed problems associated with the work setting. The role of the psychiatrist in the work organization has been discussed in connection with both the clinical program (see pp. 57ff) and the organizational programs (see pp. 79ff).

PSYCHOANALYSTS

Unlike the titles of physician, psychiatrist, and psychologist, which are defined in laws that specify the requirements for licensure, the designation of psychoanalyst is not legally protected. Consequently, any individual with any kind of training, or none at all, is free to adopt the title "psychoanalyst."

Actually, however, there are many highly reputable psychoanalytic institutes that offer specialized training in analytic theory and methods. Some restrict their admissions to physicians who have satisfactorily completed medical school and had some basic general experience. Others are open to persons without the M.D. degree—e.g., psychologists, social workers, etc.—who can meet their educational requirements for admission. As a rule, these institutes require three to five years of academic work and supervised training and a "control analysis" in which the would-be analyst becomes the patient. There are several groups organized to examine psychoanalysts and certify that they meet certain minimum requirements of training and experience. The American Examining Board of Psychoanalysis maintains a roster of those it has certified; it includes chiefly analysts who are not psychiatrists, most of whom are social workers. Psychiatrists who have completed analytic training are usually registered with one of two organizations: The American Psychoanalytic Association and the American Academy of Psychoanalysis. Each of these will respond to inquiries about whether particular analysts are included in their roster and will provide information about their backgrounds and qualifications.

PSYCHOLOGISTS

There are about 71,000 active psychologists in the United States, more than half of whom have earned a doctoral degree and the remainder a master's degree. In most states, the higher degree, obtained after a four-to-five-year program of graduate education and training, is a requirement for a license to provide direct clinical services. Psychologists work in many fields—education, research, private practice, consulting—and in a variety of subspecialties. Clinical psychologists deal with human problems in a variety of settings, including stress-management programs in work organizations. Industrial psychology is a subspecialty particularly concerned with such matters as the organization of work, job satisfaction, employee morale, and training programs for employees. Personnel psychology is a subspecialty that focuses more narrowly on matters relative to the hiring, placement, and promotion of employees.

Like psychiatrists, many clinical psychologists embrace a particular theory or system of therapy that forms the exclusive basis of their activities. Most, however, employ an eclectic approach. The American Psychological Association, with about 31,000 doctoral members and about 10,000 associate members with a master's degree, is the largest professional organization in this field. It will respond to questions about whether and how psychologists are listed in its national directory and will provide information about the background and qualifications of any member.

Organizations seeking a mental-health professional employ psychologists more often than psychiatrists. There are many more of them with the requisite skills, many have special training in dealing with the work setting and its problems, and they generally do not command the high salaries required to attract a psychiatrist. In many situations, they perform no less effectively than the psychiatrist.

SOCIAL WORKERS

By far the largest professional group providing counseling services is social workers. Their traditional focus on helping clients to understand their problems and to cope with them through the appropriate utilization of family and community resources makes them particularly effective in dealing with people problems in the work setting. When this is coupled with an acquired competence in counseling, they become an excellent resource for evaluation, direct treatment, and referral. Their major handicap is the much too prevalent tendency to equate "social worker" with "welfare worker." This conjures up an image of a worker with a large case load whose role is to certify people for welfare benefits. This negative image suggests that social workers are suspicious, prying bureaucrats, depressed and angered by the demands of the clients, and that everything they do represents "charity." Although long since outmoded, this image does persist. However, once installed and functioning, the social worker has no difficulty in erasing it from minds of employees and managers alike.

Most social workers work in health-care institutions and community agencies, although there is a growing interest in independent clinical practice. They have a long tradition of serving in work organizations and the number entering this area is growing.

The National Association of Social Workers maintains a "Clinical Register" listing members who have met the minimal standards that it has established for the various categories of service. Another resource is the National Registry of Health Care Providers in Clinical Social Work which lists social workers who offer psychotherapy.

MARITAL AND FAMILY COUNSELORS

In almost every statistical tabulation of the kinds of problems presented by troubled employees, marital and family difficulties are found at the top. In many cases, they are stimulated or aggravated by factors in the work setting: too much overtime, irregular hours, extensive travel, the two-career family, etc. In most instances, they are personal and private in the home. Nevertheless, almost invariably, they are brought to the workplace where they inevitably affect performance and productivity. A large part of the psychotherapy provided within the work setting deals with these problems and, although only a few designated marital counselors are employed by organizations, some competence in this field is usually required.

A major drawback to providing marital and family counseling in the workplace is that the former involves both husband and wife and the latter all family members. Since, as a rule, only one is an employee, the others are required to come to the work premises. This may present difficulty in that it may be inconvenient and it may not be considered a neutral environment.

Another problem is the lack of any mechanism for assuring the competence of the counselor. Anyone can set up shop as a marriage counselor and offer treatment. The American Association of Marital and Family Counselors has set minimum standards for its members and is ready to provide information on therapists specializing in this field.

REFERENCES

Pelletier, K. R. (1977). *Mind as Healer, Mind as Slayer: a Holistic Approach to Preventing Stress Disorders.* New York: Dell.

Warshaw, L. J. (Sept. 1977). The malpractice problem and the occupational physician. *J. Occup. Med* **19**:593–597.

6

PROTOTYPE
CLINICAL PROGRAMS

Increasing numbers of work organizations are sponsoring in-house units or arrangements to provide stress-management services to their employees. These vary with the organization's size, affluence, and degree of concern about its employees' psychosocial well-being. In many, they are woven into the fabric of an existing employee health unit; in others, they function more or less independently. Their effectiveness depends on the kinds and quality of services they provide, the capabilities and interests of the persons staffing them, and the kind of reputation they earn among the employees they would serve.

For the most part, they focus initially on the kinds of person-centered activities that comprise the clinical and the preventive programs. Almost inevitably, however, if their staff is properly motivated and not too timid to approach appropriate persons in management, their observations of the influence of work-related factors on the health and well-being of the employees they treat impels them to reach out for the activities characterized as the organizational program. The following prototypes indicate in a very general way how these programs may operate.

EMERGENCY-COUNSELING PROGRAMS

The concept of a round-the-clock, trouble-shooting, emergency-counseling service has been advocated for at least several decades by those concerned about individuals in difficulty who are unable to procure timely professional advice. Originally, such services were intended for suicidal individuals as a response to the "cry for help" that the intended self-destruction frequently signifies. With the spread of drug abuse, they were adapted as sources of emergency assistance and sympathetic understanding for individuals who had overdosed or were having a "bad trip."

In about 1970, what is believed to be the first worker-oriented program was initiated at the Utah Copper Division of the Kennecott Copper Corporation. It has been eminently successful; employees who received counseling through this service are reported to have reduced their rate of absenteeism by 33 percent and their utilization of medical services by 55 percent in comparison with a group of employees who rejected such help. This produced a decrease in the cost of their nonoccupational accident and sickness insurance of 74.6 percent. As a result, similar programs have been introduced in over 100 business organizations and a number of firms have been organized to supply such services on a contract basis.

The program goes under a variety of labels to avoid the stigma associated with such terms as "mental" or "emotional." One, known as "INSIGHT" (an acronym to make the phone number by which it is reached easy to remember), provides a telephone answered around the clock, seven days a week, by a person trained in counseling and familiar with treatment resources available in the area and the persons in the organization who can provide answers to questions that might be asked about company policies and procedures. Calls are taken not only from employees, but also from members of their families. The problems presented cover a broad spectrum, ranging from acute mental illness to a consumer complaint. Many callers seek advice about personal financial transactions or explanations of the benefits provided by the organization. Disturbed marital relations and problem children usually account for about one-third of the calls. Fewer than one-third are generated by difficulties arising in the workplace. However, except for the rare calls that seem to test whether they will really be answered and those which are entirely frivolous, most of them touch on problems that seem sufficiently bothersome to affect work performance.

Often, the problems are resolved in the initial phone call. In many cases, however, the individual will be given an appointment for a face-to-face meeting with a counselor for a more careful evaluation and referral to an appropriate resource. These meetings are usually held away from the organization's premises to emphasize their confidentiality and to avoid the fear of running into coworkers or a supervisor. "We will meet in their houses, our office, a street corner," reports a Kennecott manager. "We've even met people in graveyards." While these are scarcely auspicious surroundings for professional counseling, they do emphasize the availability that is the keynote of these programs.

In contrast to the community "hot lines" that are frequently served by well-intentioned nonprofessional volunteers, the troubled-employee services are usually staffed by social workers or other health professionals who have had at least some formal training in counseling. For example, the Kennecott program was developed and supervised by a qualified social worker (who now has his own firm which sells such programs on a contract basis to more than a dozen companies) and staffed by part-time graduate students who were completing their training in psychology or social work at a nearby university. The service emphasizes social interaction rather than formalized therapy; it is careful to set only direct, very short-term goals rather than attempting to grapple with problems that exceed its capacity and the capabilities of its staff. Acceptance of this service is signaled by the endorsement of the Kennecott program by that company's nineteen unions, and by reports from virtually all of its prototypes that they are used each year by about 15 or 20 percent of the employee groups to which they are made available. Of special advantage is the fact that they are relatively inexpensive.

On the other side of the balance, it should be noted that these services are limited, generally superficial, and sometimes even casual. Sometimes, there is justifiable concern over the qualifications of the staff and the closeness of their supervision. Detailed knowledge about the operations and emotional environment of the sponsoring organization is often lacking; under these circumstances, advice about a particular work situation may be impractical or even disruptive. Finally, they serve only individuals who contact them, with little or no opportunity for follow-up or preventive interventions.

EMPLOYEE-COUNSELING PROGRAMS

Stress-management programs in organizations that do not maintain an inplant medical facility are usually found in small to medium-sized organizations whose size and budget limitations preclude a more comprehensive approach to employee health. They are usually engaged in white-collar or light manufacturing activities where accidents and environmental hazards do not represent a major problem.

These programs are usually more than adequately justified on the basis of concern about absenteeism, turnover, lost productivity, and declining performance attributable to emotional and interpersonal difficulties. They often result, however, from the interest of key executives following a confrontation with such problems in themselves, family members, or close business associates, or their participation in one of the seminars or workshops on stress and emotional health whose popularity is growing so rapidly. Whatever the reason, an enthusiasm for stress-management activities can be counterproductive if it impels an individual to become an amateur psychiatrist, meddling in problems for which he or she has no training and probably little competence. When such individuals fall into the trap of implicitly using the authority of their position in the organization to dictate the involvement of employees and to command compliance with their recommendations, they can be disruptive. I recall one instance when such an individual became so committed to his therapeutic ventures that he allowed them to intrude on his work responsibility to the detriment of his own position.

In its simplest form, the organization arranges for a psychiatrist or psychologist to hold meetings with managers and supervisors in which he or she instructs them in the general principles of stress management and how to recognize the signs and symptoms of difficulty. A contract is then negotiated that requires the psychiatrist to reserve some time each week for appointments with employees who come spontaneously or at the suggestion of a supervisor. In some organizations, these appointments must be arranged by a designated manager, often someone in the personnel department. It is important that this procedure remain a conduit for rather than a barrier to such appointments.

As a rule, the contract provides a limited number of appointments at the expense of the organization. If more prolonged treatment is required, the employee becomes responsible for the cost with the assistance of whatever mental-health benefits are provided under the organization's group-insurance coverage. Unless there is a dearth of local treatment facilities, it is probably prudent for psychiatrists to limit their involvement with employees to the level covered by the contract, referring those requiring more help to other resources in the community.

In 1975, after careful investigation and planning, the Southern Connecticut Gas Company, based in New Haven with about 600 white- and blue-collar employees, launched such a program in conjunction with two Family Service agencies serving their headquarters area: Family Services of Greater New Haven and Family Services-Woodfield. These agencies are affiliated with Family Service Agencies of America, Inc., a network of more than 300 such agencies in the United States and Canada, and both are beneficiaries of the United Way, to which the company and its employees contribute.

The program was initiated by a series of comprehensive three-hour sessions in which the company's ninety supervisors were given details of the operation of the program and taught what to do when deterioration of on-the-job performance or other signs of difficulty appeared. The company's two local unions endorsed the program and sent representatives to the training sessions.

When an employee's performance drops to the point where disciplinary action is mandatory, the supervisor suggests that he or she may need professional help and advises a voluntary visit to the personnel department, guaranteed to be private and confidential. The personnel department then arranges a meeting off the premises with a qualified social worker from one of the two participating agencies in which the problem is identified and a course of action planned. The agency may work with the employee directly, provide ongoing counseling, both individual and family, or refer the individual to another agency or a treatment facility. The company is notified only that the employee is keeping the appointments, all details of the problem and the nature of treatment being held confidential. The disciplinary action is stayed and the employee continues to work while treatment progresses.

The company pays the agency's fee for the initial "intake" interview, but all additional costs are borne by the employee or the employee's health insurance. For problems not covered, the agencies have established a sliding-scale fee schedule under which the employee is charged an amount related to income.

The cost of this program is indeed nominal. It required about six months to develop the design and to negotiate the details of the program with the Family Service agencies. The training sessions for the supervisors and union officials involved a labor-hour cost of only about five thousand dollars. The only continuing cost is the fee for the initial interview when an employee enters the program.

The results have more than met expectations. Within the first two months, nine employees had enrolled in the counseling program, and a year later, eight were still on the payroll although each had been considered in a "last chance" category (Reardon, 1976).

In Newton, Massachusetts, the Charles River Counselling Center, a proprietary unit, has been providing comparable programs to a number of companies, including banks, offices, assembly-line operations, and retail stores. The Charles River Counselling Center's programs, however, are conducted on the premises during regular working hours.

Although some tailoring is done to the characteristics of the organization and its employee population, its programs are quite similar. Following a series of announcements describing the program and detailing the professional qualifications of its staff, meetings are held with employees to introduce the staff and explain what they will be doing. These are supplemented by articles in the companies' internal publications.

The program staff is assigned an office in which they spend one or more several-hour sessions each week seeing employees and members of their families who voluntarily seek their help. The company pays the entire cost of a limited number of visits—as many as eight—with any additional treatment to be provided off-site at the expense of the employee or the employee's health-insurance program. These individuals either continue their treatment at the Charles River Counselling Center or are referred to other resources in the area.

The Charles River Counselling Center's therapists attempt to draw a sharp line between the individual treatment they provide and organizational consulting which they attempt to avoid. To become involved in the company's operations and policies would, they fear, threaten the credibility they are striving to establish with its employees. They maintain strict confidentiality with respect to their activities, providing the company only with periodic reports of such statistical data as number of patients, number of visits, numbers of employees and family members, and numbers in continuing therapy at the center or elsewhere.

To compensate for the lack of familiarity of the center's therapists with the occupational environment and to promote higher standards of performance, they meet twice each week. One meeting is devoted to scheduling and other procedural matters. The other is devoted to peer review in which each therapist reviews all of his or her cases and is benefited by the observations and suggestions of his or her colleagues (Thacher et al., 1977).

In sum, it seems quite evident that programs of this kind are worthwhile, even though the benefits may be difficult to measure with precision. By assuring availability and covering at least the initial costs, they do encourage earlier utilization by troubled employees, thus their problems may be more quickly and less expensively resolved. The usual lack of experience of their staffs with work-related problems and organizational matters means that they are generally limited to personal and family difficulties, but since it has been found that most employee problems originate outside of work, they still have a broad range in which to function. A major advantage is their low cost and the fact that they do not require commitments to "permanent" personnel.

EMPLOYEE HEALTH UNITS

Employee health units were originally created to provide prompt, effective emergency care to employees who were injured or taken ill while at work. Their mission expanded to include such activities as preemployment examinations to identify individuals with medical impairments that dictate appropriate restrictions in placement or work assignment; verification of the illness of absent employees to minimize abuse of absence privileges and benefits; monitoring and controlling exposures to toxic agents such as gases, dusts, heat, noise, and radiation; and periodic medical examinations for the identification of early signs of illness so that preventive measures can be instituted. Rehabilitation of injured or sick workers became an important function in some employee health units; this involved adaptation of machines, instrument panels, and production methods that often benefited workers without impairing the operation of the machines.

By and large, attention remained focused on the physical health of workers and the control of potentially toxic exposures in the work environment that might affect it. Psychological factors were probed to reduce losses from the proverbial "three A's": accidents, absenteeism, and alcoholism. Individuals involved in repeated accidents were studied to define the characteristics that made them "accident-prone." The concept that most "unnecessary" absences represented malingering led to elaborate monitoring systems to deter such abuses. The discovery that job jeopardy made alcoholism programs in the workplace far more successful than their counterparts in the community and growing awareness of the pervasiveness of this problem stimulated their adoption by industry.

A few psychiatrists became involved, but their attention was largely directed to the treatment of individuals with mental illness who happened to turn up in the work force. They also promoted the acceptance by industry and the return to work of recovered mental patients. Much of their time was spent in teaching the rudiments of psychiatric techniques to the physicians and nurses staffing employee health units so that they might identify and deal with mental-health problems earlier and more effectively.

In recent decades, gradually and in very spotty fashion, the mission of the employee health unit has broadened in response to a number of concurrent factors reflecting newer knowledge and social change. The definition of health now includes not only physical, mental, and social well-being, but also concepts of optimal functioning and individual satisfaction. The barriers between the medical, behavioral, and social sciences have been eroded to permit sharing the fruits of countless studies of the influence of psychosocial factors on the performance and productivity of workers and the effects of the emotional and social as well as the physical stresses of work and the work environment on their health. Today, the mission of the comprehensive employee health unit goes far beyond the band-aid and aspirin dispensing activities of its predecessor to include a broad range of responsibilities not only to the individual worker but to the employer and the community (see Table 6.1).

It must be acknowledged that all of these goals are appropriately addressed in only a few of today's employee health units, those maintained by larger, wealthier, and more socially conscious employers. However, although they may be assigned varying priorities dictated by the nature and location of the plant and the particular constellations of problems presented by its work force, they are usually kept in mind wherever the employee unit is staffed by better trained and motivated health professionals.

Employee health unit staffed by an occupational nurse

Many small and medium-sized organizations maintain an employee health unit staffed by an occupational nurse, usually with a nearby

TABLE 6.1 *The mission of occupational medicine** *

To meet its fundamental objective of maintaining the health of the work force, the modern employee health program seeks to:

- Place each worker in a job that he/she can perform without endangering himself/herself, coworkers, or the public.

- Monitor job tasks and the work environment to identify materials and activities that might be harmful and recommend changes that would eliminate or satisfactorily control such hazards.

- Identify workers whose individual characteristics or prior work exposures make them especially susceptible to a particular occupational hazard and recommend appropriate steps to control it or to protect them from its influence.

- Monitor the health of workers on all levels to identify as early as possible any potential or developing indications of disease, occupational and nonoccupational, and recommend appropriate action to eliminate or minimize them.

- Assist employees to maintain satisfactory records of attendance and productivity by identifying and correcting health-related factors responsible for absenteeism, impaired work performance, and poor work discipline.

- Recommend to management appropriate modifications in the organization of work, personnel relations, benefit program, and workplace amenities that will enhance employee health and well-being.

- Provide educational and training programs to enable employees to recognize and cope with potential work hazards, and to encourage their acceptance of preventive health services and the adoption of healthful lifestyles.

- Enhance the accessibility, availability, and quality of community health care resources and encourage their appropriate utilization by employees and their dependents.

- Assist management to develop and implement policies and programs to support the health-related aspects of corporate social responsibility to its personnel, its customers, and the community.

* Adapted from L. J. Warshaw (1978). Employee health services for women workers. *Preventive Medicine* 7:385–393.

physician providing backup support and some sort of supervision. For many decades, long before the terms "nurse practitioner" and "physician's assistant" were coined, occupational health nurses have been providing a wide range of health services. These include first aid for accidental injuries and, with the blessing of "standing orders" authorized by a physician, the evaluation and treatment of minor illnesses brought to the workplace or originating during working hours. Nurses generally develop intimate knowledge of the work processes and work activities, and frequently are able to identify those associated with frequent accidents and illness and call them to the attention of the appropriate manager.

Their real forte, however, is usually counseling. Many occupational nurses come from public health and community agencies where they have had a thorough indoctrination in "people" problems. This is often supplemented by training in counseling provided in the many workshops and seminars offered by the American Occupational Health Nurses Association and its local component groups and by some universities. Frequently, this is done with the organization allowing time off for this purpose and paying not only the tuition charge, but also the costs of travel and living expenses.

It does not take long for occupational nurses to become well acquainted with most of the employees, especially those who are frequently in difficulty, and to tune in to the organization's "grapevine" through which they may acquire much helpful, albeit often exaggerated and distorted, information. When nurses have the interest, the energy, and the intellectual capacity, they serve admirably as a "first line of defense" against excess stress and decompensation. Wisely, they usually establish communication with the employees' personal physicians, but when these prove unequal to the task or are just "too busy" to bother with such problems—this happens all too frequently—nurses draw on the contacts they have made with local mental-health practitioners and agencies for appropriate referrals. Once employees are in therapy, nurses are able to follow their progress. They serve as a communication link informing the therapist about work related problems that might influence the employee's course, and advising the organization about the nature and duration of any temporary adjustments in work assignments and hours that may be necessary. Nurses often play a singularly supportive role in encouraging the employee to stay with the therapy when, as happens so often, the going gets rough or improvement seems to be too slow.

If the organization initiates the kind of counseling program described earlier, a nurse's activities can significantly enhance its effectiveness. For this reason, nurses and the units that they staff should be integrated into its activity. Nurses can serve as the "clearing house" for appointments and observe the behavior of individuals under treatment between appointments. With adequate training and the supervision of the psychiatrist or psychologist directing the program, nurses can take on specific counseling assignments, thereby permitting the program to serve a larger case load.

Equal in importance to what occupational nurses can do is what they should not do. Too often, as the only health professional, the organization will expect nurses to handle virtually every kind of problem themselves. Some nurses, impelled by a compulsion to do good, have stirred up a great deal of trouble by going beyond their training or becoming overly involved with a particular employee's problems professionally or, even worse, personally. A fundamental part of all good training programs and a special function of a supervising physician or psychiatrist is instilling awareness of the limitations of the nurse's capabilities. It is important that this be appreciated by the person to whom the nurse reports and generally understood throughout the organization so that when the nurse is forced to draw that line, it will not be construed as lack of interest or an unwillingness to become involved.

These programs are handicapped in some organizations by the relatively low status often accorded nurses and their activities. For example, they are sometimes assigned clerical tasks such as typing and filing to fill in their "spare" time. This is not only bad management—qualified nurses command much higher salaries than the people hired to perform such duties—but it is professionally degrading, sapping their self-esteem and morale. Even worse, by keeping nurses "busy" (these clerical chores are sometimes given higher priority than their nursing duties), it keeps them from expanding the scope and intensity of their professional activities to their full potential. In fact, it would be eminently desirable to supply nurses with clerical help to assist with the record keeping and paper work essential to the operation of the employee health unit, thereby increasing their availability for professional functions.

On the number of occasions when I was consulted by occupational nurses whose professional standards and capabilities were not respected by the organization, I suggested that they present a firmly worded statement of their position to an appropriately placed person in management. Then, if the desired changes are not introduced with reasonable promptness, I advised, they ought to resign and seek employment elsewhere. It was apparent that if they did not, their skills would atrophy and, however helpful they might be to a few employees, the program as a whole would accomplish little.

To summarize, a properly designed, professionally supervised employee health unit staffed by a single occupational health nurse can make a significant contribution to employee health and well-being in the organization whose size and budget preclude the mounting of a more elaborate program. Sometimes, such a limited program is dictated by the unavailability of physicians and mental-health professionals with adequate training and experience in the world of work.

In fact, in a number of situations, two or more organizations have arranged to share such a service, either through a common unit when they occupy the same or adjacent locations, or by having the nurse work part-time in different on-site units. Many years ago, the Central Middlesex Hospital in London pioneered in providing a kind of visiting occupational nurse service, backed by a cadre of occupational physicians in a special unit in its dispensary, to the many very small plants and shops in its immediate neighborhood.

When occupational nurses are adequately trained and supervised, they can conduct a limited but very useful stress-management program or significantly enhance and expand the effectiveness of a more comprehensive program that is introduced as a supplement to their activities.

Employee health unit staffed by an occupational physician

With the addition of a physician to the employee health unit, the potential scope of its involvement with stress-related health problems extends far more broadly. Needless to say, however, this is determined by the interest, skill, and attitude of the physician with respect to such problems, and the understanding and expectation of the organization that he or she will address them. When there is only one physician, stress-management responsibilities can be specified in the formal statement of mission that guides the operation of the unit and the physician required to have or to acquire the proficiency required to meet them. In large organizations with medical departments in which several physicians are employed, one with particular aptitude and experience may be designated as the "in-house expert" to whom such problems are to be referred.

Unfortunately, the number of properly qualified physicians working full-time in industry is relatively small and it is not increasing rapidly enough to meet the growing demand. Except for a few who combine several positions into a full-time activity, most physicians employed in organizations work part-time as an adjunct to a private practice, a teaching appointment, or research activity. They bring with them their existing capabilities and prejudices—it is no secret that many physicians not only lack competence in emotional and behavioral problems, but have an actual aversion to them and because their involvement with the organization is limited, they are often not willing or able to allocate time and energy to develop the needed skills and attitudes.

It is often more than a matter of attitude. The range of responsibilities assigned to occupational physicians, and the knowledge required to deal with them, has been growing at a very rapid rate, particularly during the last decade. Merely keeping up with the many current advances in medical science and in diagnostic and therapeutic technology has become a formidable undertaking. New knowledge of the subtle effects of low-level exposures to potentially toxic occupational hazards and their possible contribution to the genesis of such complex, life-threatening disorders as cancer, chronic pulmonary insufficiency, and liver failure has required occupational physicians to sharpen their skills in toxicology, epidemiology, and bio-statistics. The increased concern of organizations about the effects on health of their processes and products dictated by occupational safety and health laws, product liability regulations, and the pressures from their customers and the public has forced occupational physicians to spend more time dealing with the detection, evaluation, and control of potentially toxic substances and environmental pollutants. The number, frequency, and variety of employee medical examinations they perform has grown markedly; some are undertaken voluntarily, but an increasing number are mandated by regulations covering workers exposed to occupational hazards. The veritable surge of women and handicapped persons into the kinds of jobs and work situations from which they had hitherto been almost entirely excluded has precipitated new interest in ergonomics and human factors, activities aimed at modifying tools, protective equipment, and work practices to accommodate their special characteristics and susceptibilities. Small wonder, then, that the occupational physician is tempted to respond, "too busy!" to the advice that he or she become more involved in the detection and control of employees' stress-related and emotional problems.

Yet, a closer look reveals that such involvement is inescapable if the physician is to do his or her job properly. The justifiable fear of preventable (by the employer) life-threatening illness and the exploitation by all the media of the "toxin of the week" foment anxiety and anger in individuals and employee groups that, especially when accurate information is lacking about the level of the exposure and the effectiveness of its control, can make working a very stressful experience. The necessity of dealing with such situations, often on an emergency basis, in an adversarial arena frequented by bureaucrats, advocates, and evangelists can be frustrating and overly stressful to the members of the organization who have these responsibilities. The affirmative-action programs for the employment and advancement of minorities, women, the handicapped, and the aged have often been burdensome to both the individuals being helped and those who must welcome them; special programs have often been required to lower the stress levels in groups whose composition has thus been altered. Finally, growing out of new knowledge of the brain and nerve function, is the new science of behavioral toxicology, which is exploring the influence of chemicals in amounts that are not manifestly toxic on perception, integration, and reaction time in the human nervous system. Starting with their first meeting at the time of a preemployment medical examination and ending with the exit examination when the employee retires or is terminated, the occupational physician is inescapably involved with the employee's personality and behavior and the ways they are affected by the stressors encountered in the workplace.

The routine medical examinations performed by the occupational physician provide excellent opportunities for the identification of unusual susceptibility to stress and the early detection of emotional difficulties. In fact, certain examinations (e.g., preemployment, disability evaluation, etc.) can be used as a kind of stress test in which blood pressure, heart rate, skin reactions, and other observations of physiologic responses suggest how the examinee is handling the stress of concealing or emphasizing information that might influence the outcome of the examination. The history of prior illnesses that are known to be caused or aggravated by stress and the record of personal habits and life-style are useful predictors of how the individual will respond to certain kinds and levels of stress in the future. These are particularly helpful when considering recommendations about placing individuals in a work situation where stresses are known to be high and in advising them what steps they might take to cope more effectively with them if the placement is made.

This can be of particular value to the employee with a past history of emotional illness as well as one who is resuming work after a bout of decompensation. Regulations prohibiting discrimination in employment against handicapped individuals are applicable in most jurisdictions to persons who have or have recovered from an emotional illness. Simple social justice, and the fact that they often have skills for which there is a tight labor market, dictate a liberal hiring policy. Increasing experience continues to demonstrate that such individuals often have long and productive careers. While the seriously maladjusted individual generally does not do well, particularly when subjected to the stresses of certain job situations to which he or she might be especially sensitive, many borderline individuals do make the grade when care is taken to place them in a suitable job situation and coaching in handling its stressors is provided.

It should be noted that this can rarely be accomplished in a single encounter. As a rule, the examination serves only to identify individuals who may require such help and to establish a level of personal rapport that will encourage them to return. Occasionally it may be useful for the physician to reach out to the employee's supervisor, with the employee's knowledge and explicit consent, or arrange to meet the supervisor in the employee's presence in order to share an understanding of the problem and make plans for matching any special needs with the constraints of the particular job situation.

The periodic medical examination is deficient, in my view, if it does not include an evaluation of the employee's handling of personal and job-related stresses. Even when automated multiphasic health testing is substituted for a more comprehensive "hands-on" physical examination, questions can be asked about perceived sources of stress and changes in patterns of personal habits and activities (e.g., sleep, food, drink, exercise, and recreation) that might suggest impending difficulty. Especially when trends appear on repeated examinations, data such as weight, blood pressure, blood cholesterol, and other laboratory results may present important clues. Since these may be significant while still within the arbitrarily designated limits of "normal," it is probably too much to expect the computer program or the individual tabulating the data to note and flag them. However, the person who reviews the findings with the employee to explain their significance, present any recommendations that are indicated, and answer any questions (I feel strongly that this should be a part of every such examination) should be sensitized to note such items and make further inquiries about them or refer the employee to the appropriate source for the further steps needed to evaluate their significance.

The periodic examination is usually aimed at disclosing early signs of latent or impending disease as a signal for prompt, more effective, and less costly intervention. For this reason, it is generally reserved for older employees who have had more time to develop such conditions and among whom the "yield" that is frequently cited as the justification for this exercise is higher. I concur that they are valuable in such populations. However, I would plead, their value as an instrument for primary prevention is better realized in younger age groups, provided that they are designed to probe beyond the signs of organic pathology to look for characteristics and habits that make for vulnerability to the effects of stress. Disorders in the genesis of which stress may play a significant role (e.g., hypertension, coronary heart disease, and peptic ulcer) usually take a long time to develop. While susceptibilities (risk factors) and unhealthy patterns of adapting to stress are relatively easy to identify, it may take decades for the first clinical signs of their effects to appear. Offering such examinations to a younger population provides opportunities to halt the disease process before it may have developed its own momentum and to modify potentially pernicious habits before they get too deeply ingrained. There is also a longer time to reap the benefits of their correction. Consequently, while their examination may be scheduled less frequently, I invariably advise against the total exclusion of younger employees from programs of periodic health appraisal.

One group of younger employees in whom I find these examinations especially valuable is those selected for executive training and other forms of eventual advancement. These people are usually superior physically, intellectually, and emotionally. They are also usually more ambitious, aggressive, and competitive. The years of their involvement in these programs sometimes as many as ten or fifteen—are generally inordinately stressful. Indeed, I sometimes think that these programs are deliberately designed as an elimination contest so that only the hardiest are left when the prized positions become available to them. But these are not always the best, and mere survival does not count the costs in terms of wear and tear, unhappy marriages and problem children, and the ultimate disillusion when they realize that the rewards do not really compensate for them.

These young people are lonely in a highly competitive world. Frequent changes in job assignment intended to broaden their knowledge and experience make it difficult to establish good relationships with their peers and other coworkers and deprive them of the social support available to established members of a work group. Since such changes often require relocation, they also sacrifice the stabilizing benefits of well-established relationships with friends and neighbors, church groups, and other community organizations, to say nothing of the professionals to whom they turn for help with personal and health-related concerns.

Their primary assets are time, energy, availability, and a readiness to accept assignments even when they impinge on personal and family life. Since most are married and have very young children, they often are stressed by the disparity between the standard of living to which they feel entitled, probably rightfully, and their ability to finance it with earnings that are pegged to their current rather than their potential worth. Their guilt over neglect of family and home responsibilities is compounded by frustration and anger when spouse and children dare to complain. In all, it is a most trying experience and it is no wonder that increasing numbers are opting out in favor of positions where advancement may be slower but life is less stressful and better balanced.

It need not come to that, and the periodic medical examination is a good point of attack. Lest it prejudice their advancement, these individuals are often most reluctant to acknowledge "weaknesses" or to voice dissatisfaction with any aspect of the organization and the course that has been laid out for them, even to a physician. Nevertheless, gentle but persistent inquiry by a physician with some skill in interviewing and a knowledge of this syndrome will generally uncover the full picture. Counseling about revising time schedules and work habits, patterns of social and recreational activities, and relationships in the home is frequently successful in improving current well-being and effectiveness and in preventing serious physical and emotional difficulties in the future.

Even better, I have known instances in which the occupational physician, having noted replication of this pattern in several individuals, has brought it to the attention of those managing these programs. Some have expressed surprise, claiming complete ignorance of these effects of a traditional program; others have acknowledged that at least some of the pressures were deliberate tactics to "toughen" and to test the trainees. In both types of situation, revisions of the program to lower the stress levels and to place greater emphasis on human values not only helped the trainees, but seemed also to make the program more effective.

Attention to potentially undesirable effects of work-related stress is important not only during scheduled examinations, but with every employee contact. Even accidental injuries—especially when they are repeated—should raise the possibility that stress was part of their cause. Incidentally, the importance of a thorough investigation of the circumstances surrounding each accident is highlighted by the occasional discovery that the injured employee was an innocent bystander and the accident was really caused by the behavior of a coworker.

A carefully kept individual medical record that is reviewed periodically is an essential tool. Clusters of visits for repeated minor functional complaints such as headache, backache, dysmenorrhea, and gastrointestinal symptoms frequently are signals of emotional difficulty, the cause of which may lie in work-related stress. Similarly, the abrupt cessation of repeated visits by an employee may indicate not a "cure" but that the employee either is "taking his business elsewhere" or has found a new, perhaps more unhealthy way of expressing his or her difficulty. The correct explanation should be of interest to the occupational physician. In any case, it emphasizes the value of a well-kept record and a follow-up whenever its periodic review suggests that it might be profitable.

Many accomplished occupational physicians handle stress-related problems and emotional difficulties as a matter of course, casually including them in the sum total of their responsibilities. This is entirely appropriate: To segregate employees with such problems could be perceived as stigmatizing. I recommend, however, that these cases be analyzed separately and the procedures for handling them and the statistics derived be set down on paper as the "Stress-Management Program" or some other designation. There would obviously be overlaps if the other activities were similarly separated—for example, a single employee encounter might turn up under two or more "Programs"—and care should be taken to avoid misunderstandings by pointing this out if these documents are to be circulated. The purpose of this exercise is to force physicians to formalize and systematize their approach to specific problems and to provide a structure for evaluating its effectiveness. It would also be useful in training and supervising the medical staff and suggesting the kinds of prearrangements that should be made with likely outside referral resources. Also, it would be a valuable instrument for obtaining the understanding and endorsement of the program from management and any involved labor unions. Work-related stress problems and the complaints of employees resulting from them are frequent issues in grievances and labor-management disputes. A formally outlined program could serve as a guideline to the physician and staff to assure their focus on the health and professional aspects of these problems and as an anwer to efforts to involve them in their nonmedical considerations.

As with the occupational nurses, the effectiveness of physicians in this field can be enhanced by supplemental education and training. Organization-sponsored participation in the seminars and workshops offered at the annual American Occupational Health Conference and courses specifically designed for the occupational physician such as those provided by the Levinson Institute in Cambridge, Massachusetts, and professional societies such as the American Academy of Occupational Medicine, the American College of Physicians, and others, would be a splendid investment.

The employee health unit with a staff psychiatrist

When a psychiatrist or psychologist is added to the staff of an employee health unit, usually on a part-time basis, its stress-management program expands further in capacity and scope. The availability of a higher level of expertise enhances not only the accuracy of the diagnostic evaluations, but also their credibility both among the troubled employees and management. It also lessens the dependence on outside consultants who may not always be available or conveniently located and often lack familiarity with the organization's internal operations, barriers to involvement in therapy that can balk its acceptance by employees who initially resist it.

To avoid preemption of their time by a few individuals, staff psychiatrists limit their therapeutic involvement to problems that can be resolved in a few visits. When longer treatment is needed, employees are usually referred to professional colleagues or to community agencies. If staff psychologists maintain a private practice, they may be tempted to see these individuals in their own offices; in fact, the individuals often request it in favor of establishing another relationship. However, as long as other resources are available, it is generally prudent for staff psychologists not to accept anyone connected with the organization as a private patient.

If staff psychologists spend all of their time seeing employees referred to them by the staff or by themselves, the organization will not receive the full benefit of their services. A portion of their time should be reserved for scheduled meetings with the medical staff. Reviews of current cases can be used as a springboard for sensitizing the staff so that they will be alert and receptive when the more subtle forms of emotional difficulty arise. They will also enhance their ability to resolve simpler problems without referring them to the psychiatrist.

It is not easy to find a psychiatrist for such a position. Many are fully committed to a private practice or an affiliation with a clinic or community agency. Some are reluctant to accept the limitations and constraints inevitably imposed on practice within a work organization. As a rule, psychiatrists have little familiarity with organizational life—for them to be effective, this deficiency must be remedied. Some psychiatrists with excellent backgrounds and reputations are found to be overly committed to a particular theory of psychodynamics or to a certain mode of therapy. Such a doctrinaire attitude would seriously hamper the emotional-health program; I would urge that such individuals be rejected in favor of a psychiatrist who has an essentially eclectic approach.

In some organizations, the stress-management program functions independently of the employee health unit, often in the personnel department. This happened quite inadvertently in one organization that had hired a clinical psychologist to design and operate a psychological testing program to guide personnel decisions. Almost inevitably, he began counseling a few individuals informally and, as his reputation spread within the organization and as the utilization of psychologic testing declined, he found himself operating a full-fledged counseling program.

The personnel department is a natural place for a counseling program. Personnel relations fundamentally involve attitudes and behavior and, as has been indicated frequently, employees involved in disciplinary actions are more often than not individuals who are acting out their emotional difficulties. Employees turn to the personnel department for information about the organization's policies and benefits and are usually most receptive to advice about the problem that generated the inquiry. Many personnel departments offer vocational counseling and career guidance, deal with the problems of relocation, and provide programs of preretirement counseling. They often include in their staffs individuals with special training and experience in counseling or add social workers or clinical psychologists with proper professional qualifications and credentials.

While stress-management programs based in personnel departments function quite well in some organizations, they are often handicapped by being too closely tied to the disciplinary arm of management. The essential threat that disciplinary measures will be invoked if the employee fails to perform satisfactorily (which so often is a potent stimulus to the proper confrontation and resolution of the problem) often gets in the way of effective therapy since the same people are involved. There is also the fear that details of the employee's stress-related difficulty will find their way into the personnel file and affect his or her future with the organization. The well-established employee health unit (unless it also functions as part of the personnel department) is generally perceived as a neutral ground or sometimes even as a potential advocate.

In some organizations, two counseling programs are maintained: one in the personnel department and other in the employee health unit or operated independently. Since it is impossible to draw a sharp line between problems involving personnel matters and those that can be classified as stress-related, emotional, or medical, and since it may be inadvisable to require an employee to separate them, a considerable extent of overlap is inevitable. It is essential, therefore, that a close collaboration be established; this is usually more effective when it is formalized in some form of documentation that will serve as an on-going guideline for this relationship. The personnel staff must become fully acquainted with the resources, interests, and attitudes of the stress-management program, while the stress-management staff must be thoroughly familiar with the capabilities, activities, and constraints of the program in personnel. Procedures for cross-reference should be designed and mechanisms established for the exchange of information without violating its confidentiality. When such a working relationship is successfully maintained, the interests of both the employee and the organization are likely to be well served.

In summary, the addition of a psychiatrist or psychologist to an in-house stress-management program enhances both the effectiveness and the authority of its activities. It reduces the dependence on outside consultants for more expert evaluation of troubled employees and facilitates the referrals that must be made. In addition to seeing employees, the psychiatrist improves the capability of the health unit staff by providing continuing training in the identification and handling of stress-related and emotional difficulties.

REFERENCES

Reardon, R. W. (Jan.–Feb. 1976). Help for the troubled worker in a small company. *Personnel* 53:50–54.

Thacher, F. J.; P. Esmiol; H. R. Ives; and B. Mandelkour (Dec. 1977). Can on-site counselling programs aid workers, reduce health costs? *Occupational Health & Safety* 46:48–50.

7

ORGANIZATIONAL PROGRAMS

Organizational stress-management programs are based on the concept of the organization as a living system that needs guidance in deploying and coordinating its resources to cope more effectively with its ever-changing environment, both internally and externally. They are an extension of the clinical programs discussed earlier.

The relationship between the organizational program and the clinical program is similar to that between a public-health agency and the practitioners, clinics, and other facilities that provide direct health services to individuals. When an employee's productivity is impaired by work-related stressors or some other source of emotional difficulty, the clinical program, comprising the in-plant unit supplemented by off-site resources, seeks to relieve his or her distress and restore his or her functional capacity. But when numbers of employees present problems in patterns which suggest that the emotional climate of the workplace might be a causative or contributory factor, the remedy lies in actions that only the organization may take. Statistics often suggest the outset of an "epidemic," and the "public-health measures" to identify and control its sources are fundamental organizational responsibilities.

Further, many preventive programs aimed at individuals in the work setting are feasible and economical only when conducted on an organizational basis. They are sometimes mandated by the growing body of laws and regulations specifying what an organization shall or may not do in relation to hiring, placement, and protecting employees from safety and health hazards in the workplace. Union negotiations and the realities of the labor market determine what the organization should provide its employees in terms of earnings, fringe benefits, and workplace amenities. Problems arising from job assignments and work practices are resolved by union negotiation or the grievance mechanism. Currently, however, stimulated by the emerging concepts of corporate social responsibility and the realization that a happy work force is more productive, many organizations are going even further. Adopting the World Health Organization's definition of health as more than the mere absence of disease, they are expressing concerns about their employees' psychosocial well-being and initiating efforts to make work an enriching, fulfilling, and satisfying experience.

Often, however, the organizational program is undertaken to assist the organization as a functional entity rather than as a community of individual employees. This is an era of very rapid technological, social, political, and ideological changes, all of which place great stress on the organization and those who manage it. In addition to the stress of producing and marketing products and services in today's hectic economic climate, organizations must now allocate extensive resources to coping with the inconsistencies in the laws and regulations expressing conflicting public policies and with the frustrations of dealing with the bureaucratic mechanisms created to implement and enforce these policies. The markedly increased stressfulness of dealing with suppliers and customers in today's business environment is compounded by pressures from consumers, environmentalists, community action, and the many other kinds of advocacy groups to which organizations must be responsive.

In addition, organizations are being rocked more frequently by internal changes. Takeovers, divestitures, and changes in leadership are often accompanied by extensive reorganizations. Changes in organizational directions, new product lines, rapid growth, wind-down, cut-back, and relocation are frequent stressful crises. These are difficult enough to weather in a healthy organization. They are especially stressful, however, when the organization's ability to adapt to change has atrophied. In such instances, an entirely new orientation to its environment and radically different ways of coping with it may have to be developed.

It is important to emphasize that the organizational program does not resolve these problems. It is the responsibility of management to appraise them and to design and implement the solutions. In other words, management decides *what* to do. The role of the organizational program is to assess *how* to do it, to examine how the organization functions as a living entity and identify areas of ineffective integration and maladaptation. The program helps managers to understand how individuals and segments of the organization react to significant change and to evaluate the relative merits of alternative strategies for building organizational commitment and dealing with resistance. Most of all, it provides insights that help to resolve the inevitable conflicts found in organizations: those between and among groups, departments, divisions, and the various levels of management; those between individuals in key managerial positions; and those between the organization itself and factors in its internal or external environment. As Preston K. Munter, M.D., (1977) longtime psychiatric consultant to the Itek Corporation in Lexington, Mass., and Director of the Harvard Law School Health Service, puts it, the program deals "chiefly with the resolution of process problems as distinct from the problems of so-called substance." He goes on to point out that these process problems "frequently have more substance and may be more difficult to resolve."

Dr. Munter identifies five major sources of organization conflicts:

1 *Faculty Communications*—As in every form of human conflict, the most frequent source of organization conflict is inadequate or defective communication. It is astonishing how many top-notch, truly creative managers have difficulty in communicating ideas and instructions, and how often they fail to appreciate how their carefully polished policy statements and directives might be perceived by those to whom they are addressed. Of course, communication in an organization involves more than documents; it includes all forms of interpersonal contact (including the nonverbal) and the multidirection channels that must be established and maintained free of distortions.

2 *Defective Management Style*—Like people, organizations have individual personalities that are conditioned by the "style" of their management. These styles vary from highly centralized authoritarian dictatorships to completely free-wheeling democracies where all decisions are made by broadly representative committees. And, as in people (indeed, they usually reflect the personalities of the people in top management), these different styles are not necessarily bad. It is when they are inconsistent, uncertain, or unclear, unsuited to the nature and environment of the organization, or inflexible and maladaptive that they lead to strife.

3 *Unrealistic Expectations*—Unrealistic expectations on the part of management with respect to its employees or on the part of employees with respect to management, often, but not always, the result of faulty communications, lead to conflict, frustration, and anger.

4 *"Inhuman" Working Conditions*—Here, Dr. Munter refers not to the physical work environment (although literal uprisings can occur when an organization needlessly exploits the health and the well-being of its employees by failing to correct intolerable working conditions), but circumstances that hamper individuals' ability to lead reasonable lives on the job and away from it, and which are too disparate from current social values.

5 *Personal Problems*—When the personal problems of key individuals are sufficiently intense or sustained, they can affect the function and the integration of the organization.

To these, I would add a sixth: the inappropriate response of the organization to the advocates of new social policies within the organization and in the world in which it lives. Especially when these advocates represent an influence that cannot be ignored and are needlessly strident and unreasoning, they can have a singularly unsettling effect on the organization.

To assist in eliminating such sources of conflict, the organizational program brings a knowledge of the psychodynamics of individuals, groups, and organizations, coupled with an understanding of how the organization is structured and functions. It requires an ability to communicate without the use of jargon, a commitment to make education and training an integral ingredient of all contacts, and complete freedom from any hints of self-serving or conflict of interest. There must also be an explicit commitment to respect confidentiality and privacy.

Many organizations look to management-consulting firms to provide them with an organizational program—this occurs most often at times of acute crisis or profound changes—and many of these firms do an excellent job. They are often, however, handicapped by lack of familiarity with the organization and the subtleties of its operation, its people, and the ways these relate to each other. While they can usually supply staff with training and experience in organizational management and consulting, their people often lack expertise in the psychodynamics of stress and interpersonal relationships. Once they have won the contract and laid out what is to be done, they often assign younger, often relatively unsophisticated persons to do the actual explorations and detailed investigation on which their recommendations will be based. This can be inadvertently disruptive, especially when there is not enough time to pay adequate attention to "nerve endings" that may be exposed or to make sure that the sought-for information is accurate and complete.

There is often a remarkable similarity between the final recommendations provided by these consultants and their usually quite-accurate perceptions of the solution the client organization would find most receptive. (It has been said that this is the essence of the art of management consulting). This is not always bad. The solutions are sometimes quite obvious, but their acceptability can be enhanced by having them validated by an authority outside the organization. Also, when the solutions dictate certain actions that may not be very popular, having them suggested by an outside consultant implicitly absolves management of at least some of the responsibility for implementing them. Unfortunately, at least in my experience, this ploy is usually quite transparent and, although it may be emphasized in meetings and group discussions, few are really taken in by it.

Some organizations, again usually at times of crisis, turn to a psychiatrist, psychologist, or other mental-health professional to provide their organizational program. He or she may be a personal acquaintance (sometimes, a relative) of a top manager, someone involved in a local mental-health clinic or agency, or a faculty member at a nearby university or professional school. A number of psychiatric groups and clinics are now also seeking to provide such services. Although this can work quite well, there is often a lack of knowledge and sophistication with respect to organizational structure and function and the world of work. I have found a paucity of management skills, even in professionals who have served as department heads and clinic directors.

I recall one organization that contracted with the department of psychiatry of a local university to study some of the problems created for employees by work-related stress, to evaluate how well they were being handled by the stress-management program provided by the organization's medical department, and to suggest actions that management might take to minimize any difficulties. This department successfully operated several clinics and neighborhood programs, and had been singularly helpful to a number of the organization's employees who had been referred to it because of a variety of emotional and behavioral difficulties. There was no crisis or time pressure—a full year was allocated to the project.

A multidisciplinary team was assembled under the direction of the department head. It comprised several psychiatrists with prestigious reputations, a clinical psychologist, a social worker, and an expert in records and statistical analysis. Wisely, they decided not only to evaluate individual cases and their outcomes, but also to explore the patterns of operations and relationships within the organization. This turned out to be a new and fascinating world for them. While they more than adequately dealt with the clinical aspects of the project, they probed with great interest and diligence into those few segments of this rather large organization to which they had access. At the end—it actually took them several months longer than the allotted year—they proudly presented their findings. These were interesting, and the project team had obviously learned a great deal in the process, but, unfortunately, they contained nothing that had not already been known to the organization's medical director and, through him, the key people in management.

Another organization ran into a different problem. This was a smaller organization whose chief officer, following a trade association conference that featured several talks on stress, decided to explore the desirability of launching an organizational program. He reached out to one of the speakers at that meeting, a psychiatrist highly respected as a therapist, clinical consultant, and teacher, who had lectured most effectively on diseases caused by stress. Arrangements were made for him to visit the organization several times a week for six months during which he would interview key individuals at various levels of management to gain insight into their organizational relationships and problems. However, being a superb clinician, he kept probing their personalities and individual problems. At the end, he had a collection of magnificent case histories but he never really came to understand the organization as a functional entity. Several of the people he had interviewed went on into more intensive psychotherapy from which they undoubtedly derived some benefit, but the investment in his contract brought very little return to the organization.

I can recall more than a few instances in which a medical director also provided an effective organizational program. This requires a special mix of ingredients, the most important being the capability, interest, and energy of the medical director. It requires time that must be made available without compromising the direction of the clinical and preventive programs. It also requires that the director supplement his or her intimate knowledge of the various work settings in which the employees function with an understanding of the problems that confront the organization and the strategies being planned to deal with them. Regardless of the director's niche in the organization chart, he or she must have frequent direct access to top managers and be welcomed as an observer in their meetings and planning sessions. This must be accepted without resentment on the part of those in the chain of command through whom he or she would ordinarily be reporting.

Only sensitive, strong, and secure individuals can play this role successfully. However skilled they may become in "second guessing" management, they must resist the constant temptation to meddle. They must establish intimate relationships with top managers based on mutual respect and trust without losing their credibility as an advocate for all employees and without getting caught on the fly-paper of organizational politics. They must be aggressive enough to volunteer observations and recommendations before they are requested, strong enough to press them even when they seem to be poorly received, and secure enough to accept their rejection without considering this an injury to their self-esteem or a threat to their position.

This role is not without risk. These individuals must spread their energies over so broad a range that, without reliable assistance, they may find some ends unravelling. This venture into the art and science of management involves giving up at least some of the protection afforded by their professional status and privileges; in-plant directors relinquish the mystical authority that came with their medical diploma and license to practice. Because of their close involvement with the management team, they run the risk of becoming so identified with them that they become a target for replacement when circumstances dictate a change in organizational leadership. For example, I know one medical director whose recommendations were perceived as particularly threatening to the empire that an executive vice-president was building. Two years later, when that individual was selected to replace the retiring president, one of his first official acts was to demand the resignation of that doctor.

In a relatively few instances, the organizational program is entrusted to a psychiatrist. This happens infrequently, not because it doesn't work, but because of the small number of able and acceptable psychiatrists who are willing to venture into an area for which they were not trained. In this area, the rules are not made by psychiatrists, not even by physicians, but by laypersons. Yet, the psychiatrists I know who have entered it find it personally and professionally rewarding and derive great satisfaction from the knowledge that their success in it improves the lot of many more people than they could ever help through their usual therapeutic activities.

There are a number of caveats to be appreciated by both psychiatrists and the managers who engage them. First, time must be allowed—a year is not too long—to really get the program moving. It takes time for psychiatrists to get to know an organization, its environment, and its people, and to establish a reputation for interest, affability, and competence. They must hold rigidly to the tenets of privacy and confidentiality and yet convince individuals of their ability to use and convey without detriment to its sources information important to the organization.

Psychiatrists will inevitably find themselves pressed to counsel managers with whom they are working closely on the handling of their personal problems. This sometimes presents a serious dilemma. It is impossible to reject them, not only because of the close personal relationship, but because the difficulty may impinge on the manager's performance and role in the organizational program. The psychiatrist's professional integrity would not allow sloughing them off with superficial casual advice when he or she is aware that they need a deeper, more intensive approach. Yet, it would be distracting and time consuming to take these managers on for definitive therapy as part of the organizational program. It would be unseemly to establish a clinical practice within the organization if it already has an active clinical program—this would set up a two-tiered program, one for the rank-and-file and one for the elite, that would denigrate the former. To take on these individuals as private patients apart from the relationship with the organization presents the frequently disconcerting task of constantly deciding what portion of their contacts represents therapy for which a separate fee is appropriate and what portion is part of the psychiatrist's role in the organizational program for which he or she receives a salary or some other form of payment.

While there are general guidelines, there is no one solution that will satisfy all the variations of this situation. In the last analysis, it must be left to the integrity, judgment, and good will of the players and their sensitivity to how that solution, however it may be justified, might be perceived.

In summary, the organizational program comprises a broadening of the clinical program from concern about individuals to the problems of groups, units, or the organization as a whole, as well as a more or less separate activity that deals with the organization as a living, functioning entity. Like people, organizations often have difficulty in adapting to change and coping with stress. If properly designed and deftly directed, the organizational program can make a significant contribution to the health of the organization and the well-being of its personnel.

REFERENCES

Munter, P. K. (1977). Conflict resolution at work—the psychiatrist's role. Presented at the American Occupational Health Conference, Boston, Mass., April 27, 1977.

8
PSYCHOLOGICAL TESTING

For a time after World War II, psychological testing enjoyed a great vogue in business organizations and certain government agencies. Many organizations made a battery of tests a mandatory part of the evaluation of all applicants for employment. Some applied it only to candidates for such positions as sales, customer contacts, and executive positions, while other organizations relied on psychological tests to determine which of several employees to promote. In more than one instance, an organization contemplating an acquisition made the psychological testing of its key personnel an essential part of the decision-making process.

Some organizations hired psychologists, generally placing them in the personnel department where such testing was usually performed. Many used one or more of the consulting firms and group practices that sprang up to meet the demand for these tests. And some bought tests that had been published and assigned an employee to administer and score them on the basis of a do-it-yourself manual.

By the early 1960s, largely because of the use of invalidated tests for purposes for which they had not been designed by people who had no training in their application, testing had lost much of its popularity and its use declined. Although it is still being used in many organizations, it commands, as a rule, much less authority than it once did. Now, it is more likely to serve as a supplement to a face-to-face interview with a mental-health professional retained by the organization than as a stand-alone procedure.

It should be noted that in this discussion, I am not considering psychological testing in clinical situations or as a tool for behavioral science research. Although the same testing instruments and techniques may be employed, and the same kinds of individuals involved, the context is entirely different. In clinical situations, for example, psychological testing serves a purpose quite analogous to the use of X rays, blood tests, and other diagnostic manipulations in dealing with organic health problems: that is, to validate a suspected diagnosis and to provide baseline data against which progress can be measured.

Within the organization, the testing is applied to "normal" individuals to measure their fit against a previously constructed template of sensory and psychomotor capacities, personality characteristics, and attitudes. When the template is derived from a painstaking analysis of a job's requirements and confirmed by the testing profiles exhibited by people who have records of satisfactory performance in it (making sure that the same profile is not also found in individuals who have failed in it), the procedure can be considered a valid tool. In the majority of instances, however, the fit can be assessed far more economically by a good personnel interview and, if the record of previous employment does not demonstrate adequate capacity to do the work, a trial at performing some of the tasks the job involves may be helpful. There are instances in which the greater precision of a testing program is indicated; these include jobs in which performance failure can jeopardize public safety, such as airline pilot or air-traffic controller, and police officer, security guard, or other jobs involving the carrying of firearms. Also included are instances in which there is some uncertainty whether acceptance or rejection of a particular individual should be recommended.

It is when the template is based on stereotypes or the highly personalized notions of a particular manager that the testing becomes suspect. An experience I had some years ago in advising the management of an electronics conglomerate about a proposed plan to create an employee health unit illustrates an all-too-common situation. In chatting with the president of this organization, it became quite apparent that he had a rather rigid concept of the personal characteristics of "good" employees that served as criteria for all hiring in the middle- and upper-level job categories. "Good" employees were, he believed, aggressive, ambitious, god-fearing adherents of one of the major protestant churches who set great value on making money and the material possessions it would buy. They had little interest in the arts, cultural attainments, off-color stories, and noncompetitive recreational pursuits. To make sure that only people with these attributes were hired, all candidates for employment were required to take a battery of psychological tests selected by a consultant whose office was located some miles away from the organization's headquarters. Hiring was not centralized except for the higher executive positions. Instead, the personnel director in each subsidiary or major plant (at the time, these were scattered over several western states) received and interviewed applicants after which a member of his or her staff administered the prescribed tests. The crude scores were sent to the office of the consulting psychologist who translated them into a two- or three-page narrative description of the applicant's personality and interests. This, together with the application form and the personnel director's recommendation, was forwarded to the headquarters office where the president or his aide either confirmed or vetoed the hiring.

I arranged to apply for the same nonmedical job at each of two nearby plants concealing my identity and purpose from their personnel directors. I used the same data in the application forms—both interviews were perfunctory—and took the same battery of tests at each plant, keeping in mind the president's concepts of desirable characteristics. At the first plant, I answered each question as I imagined a person whom the president would admire would do. At the other plant, I did the exact opposite. Two days later, I got a phone call from the first plant with a job offer and an invitation to discuss a starting date and specific work assignments. I had to call the other plant to learn that I had been rejected because there were several other "more-qualified" candidates for the job I was seeking.

Subsequently, I was allowed to read the psychologist's reports, which, I would emphasize, were based only on the crude test scores. I was truly impressed by the imagination and deftness with which he had converted them into highly and explicitly detailed narrative descriptions of my personality profiles! They were not inaccurate, since I had taken pains to present myself at the very extremes of the scales. But, I wondered, how well did his profiles reflect more or less average individuals who would score close to the midpoints?

The point is that the results could easily be faked by someone with a little sophistication in taking such tests and a knowledge of what was being sought. Incidentally, there was nothing wrong with the tests, which comprised a group of widely accepted personality, attitude, and aptitude measures. The problem was that they were not really intended for this kind of use, particularly when their interpretation was of such questionable quality.

One executive who used a similar battery of tests told me that he used them only to confirm the impressions he formed in his interview of the applicant. If there was disagreement, he claimed, he tended to rely on the interview rather than the test results. The head of a commercial printing firm in Atlanta is quoted as having said, "Using tests is just a crutch. Employers who use the tests probably are too weak-minded to make decisions on their own. I just can't see that they're a substitute for good business practices" (Koten, 1978).

Critics of tests question whether inquiries about religious beliefs, sexual behavior, family matters, etc., violate our emerging concepts of individual privacy, particularly when the responses will be revealed to personnel staff and other laypersons in the organization. Although many organizations say that taking the tests is entirely voluntary, one might wonder to what extent refusal to take them would hamper the individual's chances of getting the job or the promotion.

When properly used, psychological tests can be quite valuable. They should be reserved for specific situations in which clearly defined, well-validated capabilities are required for satisfactory and safe performance. They should be administered by well-trained persons in surroundings and under conditions that do not unduly influence or intrude on the procedure. The individual should be informed of the purpose and nature of the tests. The test instruments should not be subject to bias against individuals with "different" social, cultural, and ethnic backgrounds. And, they must be scored with complete objectivity.

REFERENCES

Koten, J. (July 11, 1978). Career guidance. *The Wall St. Journal* 192:1.

PART III
REACTIONS
AND STRESSORS

9

IMPORTANT
STRESS REACTIONS

The stress reactions discussed in this chapter—alcohol and drug abuse, backache, mass psychogenic illness, and absenteeism—represent types of behavior or patterns of reaction that are encountered frequently in the work setting. In these reactions, inability to cope with stressors has a significant precipitating or aggravating role. Because this is so generally recognized, these stress reactions are frequently addressed organizationally by special programs.

ALCOHOL ABUSE

Alcohol abuse is probably the best recognized and most pervasive of the stress-related problems. The National Institute on Alcohol Abuse and Alcoholism estimates that about 10 million Americans are problem drinkers. The National Council on Alcoholism estimates that between 6 and 10 percent of employees are alcoholics. Certain occupations, mostly those that involve traveling or serving drinks, have disproportionately high numbers of alcoholics. Estimates suggest that, at any particular time, between 20 and 30 percent of the patients in general hospitals are people who drink too much. Misuse of alcohol is a factor in at least half of our motor-vehicle accidents and highway fatalities. Half the nation's homicides and one-third of reported suicides are associated with alcohol. In the third special report to the Congress on "Alcohol and Health," HEW Secretary Califano noted that alcohol is the third leading cause of birth defects involving mental retardation. "Alcohol is indisputably involved in the causation of cancer," he said. In financial terms, he added, the economic toll from alcohol problems was estimated at $43 billion in 1975, including about $20 billion in lost production and nearly $13 billion in medical costs. The latter represents over 12 percent of all health expenditures for the country's adult population (Noble, 1978). This may even be an understatement. In a study at the Peter Bent Brigham Hospital of a group of deceased patients whose postmortem examinations showed evidence of "maximally developed manifestations" of alcoholism, it was found that 90 percent had had no apparent therapy for alcoholism at any time and none had had any serious inpatient or long-term ambulatory care for alcoholism (Jankowaski and Drum, 1977). These statistics—and many more could be cited—are indeed awesome.

Alcoholism has been formally declared a "disease" (formerly, it was simply a "social problem"), and this has been reflected in legislation. The American Medical Association has widely circulated its *Manual on Alcoholism*, and a guide to physicians on *Criteria for the Diagnosis of Alcoholism*, developed in 1972 under the aegis of the National Council on Alcoholism, has been well publicized.

There is now a National Institute on Alcohol Abuse and Alcoholism. Substantial financial resources—private and public; local, state, and federal—supplemented by the efforts of volunteers in every community, are being devoted to alcohol education and research on the treatment of drinking problems.

Decades ago, a number of organizations—Eastman Kodak, DuPont, Equitable Life, Consolidated Edison of New York, and a few others—pioneered in the development of alcoholism programs for their employees. Hundreds of organizations have since emulated them. For years, the National Council on Alcoholism and its local chapters and affiliates, Alcoholics Anonymous, the National Safety Council, and other voluntary agencies have been broadcasting (literally and by all other media) information about alcoholism and offering help to organizations in dealing with it among their employees. The Association of Labor-Management Administrators and Consultants on Alcoholism (ALMACA) now has over 1,700 members who are managing and staffing programs dealing with alcohol abuse.

Labor unions have long been concerned with the problem, and many have initiated alcoholism programs for their members. Through the Labor-Management Committee of the National Council on Alcoholism they have worked with representatives of business organizations to promote early identification and more effective treatment of alcohol abuse.

To be effective, the alcoholism program must deal with the multiple facets of alcoholism:

1 *Chemical*—Alcohol is a chemical, drug, or, toxin that depresses, impairs, or permanently damages many organs and body functions, notably the brain, nervous system, liver, and gastrointestinal tract. The effect varies with the amount consumed, the period over which it is taken, and the susceptibility of the individual. It appears that some individuals may become physically addicted to alcohol, while others do not. It is not necessary to take large amounts of alcohol or to be drunk to become a victim of its effects. Relatively small amounts of alcohol in pregnant women have been shown to lead to abnormalities and impaired development in their children. In London, Dr. Beric Wright, director of the Medical Centre sponsored by the British United Provident Association which has been providing periodic health checkups for members of the Institute of Directors for almost two decades, reported blood tests indicating impaired liver function in some business executives who drank no more than a few mild cocktails a day. Happily, Dr. Wright noted, these tests returned to normal after the cocktails were stopped.

2 *Behavioral*—Ever since it was first discovered, alcohol has been used as a drug to relieve the effects of stress and anxiety and to change mood. Long before tranquilizers were discovered, it was being used (and prescribed) when stress levels became high and uncomfortable.* And, when the stress is persistent or recurs frequently, the use of alcohol becomes habitual. Even if chemical addiction does not occur, psychological dependency develops readily. Then there are two problems: the psychosocial stress in the family, the job, or the community that produced the drinking which, needless to say, is never helped by it; and its compounding by the stress produced by the alcoholic dependence and the effects of drinking on behavior and perfomance, not the least of which are the pressures to conceal them.

---

* Alcohol was undoubtedly responsible for the effectiveness of most of the popular nostrums, such as Lydia Pinkham's remedy for "female disorders," whose use was so widespread in past generations and which in one form or another are still being used today.

3 *Social*—In primitive as well as highly sophisticated cultures, drinking is a feature of social intercourse. The shared drink and drinking parties are not only obligatory elements of hospitality, but have become symbols of friendship and agreement and a traditional part of business and diplomatic relationships. Even the National Council on Alcoholism includes a "cocktail hour" in the programs of its meetings. As Edward Pessen (1978) notes in his history of American Labor in the early nineteenth century, drinking during working hours was an established part of the scene. Shipbuilders in Massachusetts had to allow their men "grog privileges" and Philadelphia artisans insisted on their late afternoon drink, passing a jug around. "Young apprentices learned to drink while they learned a trade," Pessen reports. They made regular trips to the local pub to refill the flasks journeymen brought to work with them and, on the way back, would "rob the mail" by helping themselves to a drink. In the shoemaking shops in Lynn, Massachusetts, according to historian Paul Faler, "no working man would labor unless his employer provided a half pint of liquor per day as part of his wages." Cordwainers drank their daily pint of "white eye," he reports, and each morning and afternoon an apprentice was sent out for "black stop," a mixture of rum and molasses (Faler, 1974).

These habits have come down through the years. Leadburners in Appalachia, I have been told, still insist on a daily bottle of "corn," and just a few years ago, according to a union steward, a group of house painters walked off the job when the employer refused to allow them to drink while at work. The "two martini" lunch and the after-work stop at the corner bar are established fixtures in many organizations. While a growing number of organizations prohibit any alcoholic beverages on the premises, some even in their executive dining rooms, many cite the social and cultural role of drinking as the basis for their unwillingness or inability to do anything about it.

4 *The Stigma*—For centuries, alcoholics have been stigmatized for their "moral weakness" and their aberrant behavior when drunk. They are considered a social "disgrace" and generally regarded as inefficient, unreliable, and disruptive employees. This has led to a justifiable prejudice against alcoholics with respect to hiring, placement, and promotion. In the medical world, they are considered undesirable patients because their illnesses are generally complicated and generally do not improve without permanent cessation of drinking, they frequently do not comply with recommendations and advice, they do not keep appointments, and they don't (or can't) pay their bills. Such attitudes frequently underlie the reluctance of organizations to undertake alcohol programs or to give them more than lip service. Some organizations have expressed the concern that acknowledging the presence of alcoholics in their work force by having a formal program might lead their customers to question the reliability of the goods or services they are marketing.

5   *The Cover-up*—For a number of reasons, the people around an alcoholic try to conceal his or her difficulty. They want to avoid contamination by the stigma; they are affected by the helplessness and dependency so frequently presented by the alcoholic, and the poignancy of the problem that allegedly has caused the alcoholic to drink; they rationalize that the alcoholic is a good worker and a fine person when not drinking; and they experience a touch of the "there but for the grace of God, go I" feeling. Reluctance to "blow the whistle" and guilty feelings about precipitating the sometimes inevitable disciplinary consequences deter people from calling the alcoholic to the attention of the organization. I have been frequently astonished at the extra time and effort supervisors and coworkers have been willing to donate to making up for the deficiencies and errors of an alcoholic in their unit. Managers who are reluctant to admit they made a mistake in hiring or promoting the alcoholic often seek ways to keep the problem hidden. The cover-up is abetted by the alcoholic who, least of all, wants the problem exposed. Literature and all of the entertainment media are replete with examples of the stratagems employed by alcoholics to hide their drinking. All of this makes it certain that few alcoholics will come to light in an organization without an aggressive program to persuade personnel on all levels that the purpose of identifying alcoholics is to help them and to explain why the program is so important to them and to the organization.

The ideal alcohol program is not yet available. Those in use represent an accretion of research information and experience, combined with residues of the sequence of forms of treatment that enjoyed a wave of popularity before it was realized that they were helpful only to small numbers of carefully selected individuals. These include prolonged inpatient psychotherapy, a variety of group processes, family therapy, the therapeutic community, aversive drug therapy, behavior modification, faith healing, and team approaches. This means that each program has to be custom-tailored to meet the characteristics of the people to be involved, the kinds of work they do, the organization's internal and external environments, the resources available for the program, and those in the community on which it can draw. It is more prudent to start with a modest program giving it room to grow as it takes hold, than to go all-out from the beginning. It is also prudent to avoid promises of quick results since it usually takes at least several years for the program to earn the respect and credibility needed to attract participants and at least as long for its successes to become apparent. It is especially important to emphasize that relapses—i.e., "falling off the wagon"—are to be expected in some cases. While always disappointing, they do not represent failures—the program is designed to deal with them. Finally, it is essential to avoid making any guarantees. No program is universally effective and some employees will inevitably resist salvage and be lost to the organization (sometimes, this provides the stimulus that makes the next trial of treatment successful).

The Labor-Management Committee of the National Council on Alcoholism has compiled a list of eight essential elements that can serve as a framework on which an effective program can be built. These are presented in Table 9.1.

The program should be aimed at all levels. The National Institute of Alcohol Abuse and Alcoholism estimates that 25 percent of the millions of employed alcoholics are white-collar workers, 30 percent are blue-collar or manual workers, and 45 percent are professional or management employees. Although it is more common in some ethnic groups, it is exhibited by all. This suggests that duplicate educational materials aimed at groups representing different educational, social, and language backgrounds may be more effective.

Although males preponderate in most statistics on alcoholics, the problem may well be as frequent among women. In his study of alcoholics admitted to the forty-three community alcoholism service centers in Iowa, Dr. Harold A. Mulford (1977) found that serious drinking problems tended to begin later in life for women and to progress more rapidly for them than for men. Fewer women reported problems with the police, with employers, or with finances, but they had more alcohol-related health problems. Both sexes, he found, drank for psychological effect as well as for social reasons.

TABLE 9.1 *Checklist of key program elements*

1. The company and union have a joint written policy dealing specifically with *alcoholism alone*—a policy which is known to *all* employees and which clearly delineates a positive procedure aimed at helping alcoholics to recover.

2. The company has developed specific procedures in regard to the handling and referral of employees experiencing performance problems, and line management accomplishes compliance with these procedures as a job responsibility of supervisors at all levels. Under a joint union/management program, the appropriate union representative will become involved when these performance problems arise.

3. The joint program has an effective referral system, i.e., procedures, qualified alcoholism diagnostic facilities, and personnel with the qualifications necessary to assure that alcoholics will be referred to the proper rehabilitative agencies.

4. The joint program has access to treatment facilities which are appropriate for the employed alcoholic and refers alcoholic employees to these facilities as needed.

5. The joint program has set in motion a program to train supervision and union representatives at all levels, specifically in the procedures they will follow to implement the alcoholism policy, and the procedure for making referrals.

6. The joint program has an educational component designed to inform employees regarding modern approaches to alcoholism and one which includes a complete description of the company-union policy on *alcoholism*.

7. The joint program has an effective medical recordkeeping system which assures confidentiality to the individual employee, while furnishing evidence of program effectiveness through reports on numbers of alcoholics identified and successfully motivated to accept treatment. The data utilized in these reports should permit comparison with results of other operating programs, so as to obtain meaningful measures of relative program effectiveness. These records should also provide some acceptable measure of the program's cost effectiveness.

8. The company and union have provided for third-party payment for the treatment of alcoholic employees in their group health insurance policies or other compensatory benefits.

From *A Joint Union-Management Approach to Alcoholism Recovery Programs.* New York: National Council on Alcoholism, 1976.

According to Dr. Mulford, these differences reflect the fact that the process of learning to use alcohol for psychological relief has been different for men and women. Society permits, and in many ways encourages, young men, but not young women, to drink heavily. Therefore, he suggests, men gradually drift into increasing dependence on alcohol to cope with everyday stresses, while women begin heavy drinking later in life usually in response to crises and more serious emotional problems.

One wonders how applicable these findings and interpretations would be to alcoholics in other parts of the country where different social and cultural backgrounds are more prevalent. One also wonders about the impact of women's liberation on these observations. Women are certainly drinking more—at least in public—and female drunks, once extremely rare, are seen more frequently. Will there be the same pattern of increase in alcohol-related disorders among women that was shown in the rising prevalence of heart attack and lung cancer that has accompanied their increased cigarette-smoking? At any rate, such data suggest that the alcohol program should not neglect the women in the work force.

The program should not depend on any particular form of treatment but should selectively use all that are available. Many individuals are helped only by two or more different kinds of treatment used concurrently or sequentially.

The program should make arrangements with facilities in the community to which employees can be referred for treatment. These are important even when in-house treatment programs are maintained so that breaks in continuity of treatment can be averted if, as often happens, the individual leaves or is separated from the organization. Besides, these arrangements are more economical for the organization, and its involvement strengthens the community agency.

"Job jeopardy" or the "performance approach" should be an integral part of the program. This involves the prior establishment of a set of rules and an understanding between the alcoholic and his or her supervisor that they will be invoked. These specify that specific penalties culminating in dismissal will be invoked if the employee discontinues treatment, "falls off the wagon" too many times, or fails to maintain satisfactory attendance and performance. Once this contract is made, it must be enforced. Experience has amply demonstrated that the threat of job loss and, if it happens, the consequences of losing it, provide a critical impetus to persisting with the treatment long enough for its benefits to take hold. Recovery rates in organizations where this mechanism is in use have ranged from 70 to 90 percent in contrast to the 20–50 percent recovery rate achieved by individuals receiving identical treatment from the same people but without the spur of job jeopardy.

Since most alcoholic employees exhibit poor levels of performance and/or absenteeism (Monday absences or absences on the morning after heavy drinking, especially after a mid-week payday, and prolonged lunch hours or failure to return after lunch are the most common patterns) that would ordinarily call for a disciplinary measure, the principle of job jeopardy is applied at the outset. An appropriate referral is made, and the alcoholic is firmly given the choice of starting treatment or accepting the disciplinary consequences of poor performance.

Dr. Luther Cloud, President of the National Council on Alcoholism and former director of the highly successful program at Equitable Life, says that the problem is not the treatment; the problem is motivation. "Alcoholism is a disease for which the patient does not want to be treated" (Cloud, 1974). The real question, he emphasizes, the one that goes to the core of the problem, is not how to treat alcoholics, but how to motivate them to accept and persist in treatment.

Finally, most authorities believe that the goal of treatment should be total and permanent abstinence. This view was challenged by a recent controversial study undertaken by researchers at the Rand Corporation. In this study 2,371 male alcoholics out of a population of 11,500 attending 45 community treatment centers were interviewed six months after their initial period of treatment. Improvement was found in about 70 percent, but only 10 percent had achieved the goal of six months of total abstinence. When the research team reinterviewed 1,340 of these subjects a year later, the figures were the same: 70 percent improved, but only 10 percent who had not used any alcohol for six months. The relapse rate, they found, was the same for those who tried to remain abstinent as it was for those who tried to drink socially—about 16 percent (Armor, et al., 1976). This led to the widely publicized conclusion that alcoholics could be allowed to drink again, stirring a controversy that is still unresolved.

At the National Council on Alcoholism's annual medical-scientific forum held in St. Louis in the spring of 1978, Dr. Alfonso Paredes, director of alcohol research at the University of Oklahoma, reported the results of a study of alcoholics at twenty-six treatment centers in Oklahoma. The size and method of the study was essentially similar to the Rand research. Dr. Paredes reported that those who tried normal drinking were three times as likely to relapse as abstainers; this was twice the percentage of relapse among the Rand's normal drinkers. Accordingly, Dr. Paredes concluded, there is a substantial risk of serious consequences if alcoholics are permitted to attempt social drinking.

Obviously, more research is needed. Both studies demonstrate that some alcohol abusers can resume "normal" drinking without apparent ill-effect, at least so far as their psychosocial measurements are concerned. It remains to be seen whether there might be subtle delayed toxic effects from the chemical action of the ongoing alcohol consumption. It is possible that, with the passage of more time and exposure to stressors, the rate of serious relapses among those who resume drinking will climb even much higher than was found in the Oklahoma study. It is also possible that additional research will enable us to distinguish between those for whom permanent abstention is essential and those who may be allowed to resume drinking.

For the present, I would retain abstinence as the goal of treatment in every case, but I would be consoled by the knowledge that much can be achieved even when falling short of it.

To summarize, there is widespread knowledge of the characteristics of alcoholism, its relationship to stress, its ubiquitousness in all kinds of organizations and the significant toll it extracts from them, and of reasonably effective methods of dealing with it. Yet, it remains a pervasive problem. Despite untold numbers of "cures," the population of alcoholics does not seem to be decreasing. Juvenile and childhood alcoholism is emerging as a social "cancer" that totally eclipses the more highly publicized problem of drug abuse and addiction. Physicians remain reluctant to talk to their patients about drinking and to accept responsibility for acquiring and applying available knowledge about the influence of alcohol on many of the conditions they treat. And, there are still thousands of organizations in both the private and public sectors that continue to "play ostrich" by refusing to recognize that alcoholism exists among their personnel. They take the position that it is a personal problem in which they have no right to intrude, and drag their feet in mounting an effective program to deal with it. Paradoxically, many of these organizations have devoted energy and resources to activities intended to enhance employee well-being and performance, such as job-enrichment, exercise programs, and subsidized coffee breaks.

In my view, any organization that does not have an alcoholism program, or which has not recently examined an established program to make sure that it is up-to-date and working well, is needlessly dissipating its human and financial resources and failing its responsibilities as a corporate citizen.

DRUG ABUSE

During the late 1960s and early 1970s reports of the "drug culture" made headlines daily and stirred widespread concern in nearly every community. As this is written, the furor seems to have died down, but what of the problem?

Clearly, it has not vanished. A recent national survey by the National Institute on Drug Abuse* estimated that 22 million people used marijuana last year, 7 million used prescription drugs without medical supervision, 3 to 4 million used cocaine, and 500,000 used heroin. It is well established that, although different patterns of drug taking are seen, drug abuse is found in every community, in all walks of life, at every age, and in every organization.

Like so many aspects of human and societal behavior, drug abuse is a multifaceted problem. Even when the focus is narrowed to the problems it presents in the work setting, it must be viewed from several perspectives.

First, there is the matter of legality. Organizations are rightfully concerned about the presence of illegal drugs in the workplace, especially when their premises are used as a locus for their manufacture or sale. One organization found that the lobby of its urban-skyscraper headquarters had become a market place for drug traffic, attracting drug users from distant parts of the city to purchase their supplies. Another found that some enterprising employees were using its laboratory facilities and supplies to manufacture an illicit drug. Still another, which had purchased a large tract of rural land to be developed as a vacation resort for its employees, was embarrassed by a police raid just as the caretaker was about to harvest the large crop of marijuana he had been carefully cultivating.

---

* The National Institute on Drug Abuse located in the Department of Health, Education and Welfare is concerned with prevention, treatment, and rehabilitation. Control of drug traffic still rests with the Drug Enforcement Administration in the Department of Justice. They are linked in the federal Strategy Council on Drug Abuse which includes the Secretaries of State, Defense, and HEW, the Attorney General, and the Administrator of Veteran Affairs.

Many organizations have adopted policies calling for the instant dismissal of any employees involved in such situations. Their enforcement is generally assigned to security personnel, who usually require some training in dealing with drug problems and who should always work with the local police and drug-enforcement agencies. Managers must remember that no organization is immune to such situations and should command prompt, appropriate action when one is suspected.

Habitual heavy users of drugs are not much of a problem in the work setting. Even when they succeed in getting a job, their aberrant behavior and poor performance usually dictate prompt dismissal. Neither are those who use drugs primarily for recreation or personal enjoyment as long as they refrain from indulging while at work.

There is, however, good reason for concern about the abuse of drugs among employees on all levels: the pills taken to allay anxiety and feelings of tension, the "downers"; and those taken to enhance mood, counter fatigue or improve performance, the "uppers." Such abuse seems to be on the increase. It involves illicit drugs, prescription drugs obtained illicitly, and the inappropriate use of drugs that were prescribed too casually or incorrectly. Like alcohol, these drugs impair alertness, perception, and the kinds of psychomotor functions required to drive vehicles or operate machinery with safety. As with alcohol, many individuals become dependent or otherwise habituated to their use. Then, the same patterns of withdrawn and/or disturbed behavior, impaired performance, and frequent absence are displayed. There is also the same proclivity to denial, concealment, and cover-up that is found in alcoholism.

Consequently, except for building in features to deal with particular nuances of drug abuse, the approach to its detection and treatment is identical to that used for alcoholism. In fact, a serious problem for the physician who would treat the effects on body organs and functions is that alcohol and drugs are frequently being abused simultaneously.

This suggests the desirability of a drug-abuse program being subsumed in the organization's alcohol program. Further, it emphasizes that the training activities and educational materials for supervisors and others who are expected to identify employees with these problems should caution against trying to distinguish between them. It is only necessary for them to determine that the employee has "a problem," leaving the exact diagnosis to the more qualified professionals to whom that employee will be referred.

Vocational rehabilitation of drug abusers

The employment of rehabilitated drug abusers is a responsibility which organizations should not evade. Despite the well-publicized statistics about recidivism, many addicts and drug abusers do give up their dependencies and remain drug-free. They need and deserve to be allowed back into the mainstream of society, the key to which is the opportunity to work and be self-sustaining. Not only is this much more economical than maintaining them in sequestered communities, but many have amply demonstrated their capacity to make significant contributions to society. Some may need additional education and special job training and many require support during the period of readjustment, but this is not a significant burden to most organizations. There are such risks as dropouts and failure to make the grade, but these have been shown to be no greater than in new employees hired through ordinary channels. This is a serious national problem that will never be solved unless employment opportunities are made available for those who rehabilitate themselves. It is a social and civic responsibility for every organization, one that cannot be met simply by making financial contributions to voluntary agencies involved in drug abuse, however generous they might be.

It is also a matter of self-interest. Organizations have a responsibility to their own employees who fall prey to drug abuse to continue the employment of those who are able to work while they undergo treatment and to rehire those who had to leave when they have recovered sufficiently to return. Failure to do this will destroy the credibility of the drug-abuse program and drive drug abuse further underground.

Many organizations now employ recovered drug abusers but there are still not enough jobs for them. Explaining what is required is probably best done by recounting briefly the experience of the Equitable Life Assurance Society, one of the earliest to become involved. Its program, centered in the Employee Health Services Department under the direction of Dr. Robert S. Graham, involved representatives from the Human Resources Department and all of Equitable's operating areas and scores of others ranging from the chief executive officer to the supervisors and middle-management personnel under whom the rehabilitated drug abusers were placed. To these individuals all credit for the success of the program, which has since been emulated by a number of other organizations, must be given.

The program was formally launched in 1966 at the height of the "drug crisis" when it was acknowledged that a handful of the roughly 8,000 people employed in its home office in the heart of New York City were known to be using heroin and other drugs. In sharp contrast to the current practice of seeking out and dismissing such individuals, Dr. Graham and individuals from the Personnel and Security Departments designed a pilot program quite similar to the alcoholism program the Equitable had initiated in 1959. Initially, six employees agreed to participate in the treatment and rehabilitation program that gradually was evolved. Two of the six, by the way, drug-free for more than a decade, are still Equitable employees.

As the number of drug abusers accepting treatment in the program grew, it became difficult to find facilities that would provide satisfactory treatment without unduly interfering with their ability to work. This was resolved in 1970 by an arrangement in which the Division of Community Mental Health of the Department of Psychiatry at the New York Medical College agreed to accept employees referred by the Equitable into the program it was providing to its community. This proved to be mutually advantageous: It provided effective treatment for Equitable employees while the staff acquired an orientation toward rehabilitation and work that benefited their other patients.

At about that time, the Equitable began to hire rehabilitated drug abusers referred by local community drug-treatment agencies. These included methadone maintenance programs as well as drug-free residential agencies. Despite a few successes, the initial experience was not very good.

Analysis revealed two major causes for the failures. One was the inadequacy of the vocational training and work orientation provided by some of the agencies. Their people were just not ready for work. They had not been adequately indoctrinated in and inured to the essential discipline of the workplace: coming to work regularly and on time, not wandering off to other parts of the building, and applying themselves to their assigned tasks with reasonable diligence, persistence, and effectiveness. The other was the failure of some agencies to follow their patients adequately, to report promptly to the Equitable lapses in the treatment upon which continuing employment was made conditional, and to provide the ongoing encouragement and support that was so essential in some cases.

These difficulties were largely resolved by persuading some of the agencies to upgrade their performance and provide more careful evaluation of the individuals they refer. In 1970, PACT/NADAP (Provide

Addict Care Today/National Association on Drug Abuse Problems) was organized by a group of business and labor leaders to deal with the problem of drug and substance abuse. It has developed a "clearinghouse" through which qualified job-ready individuals can be employed and assisted treatment facilities to improve their effectiveness in vocational rehabilitation. This clearinghouse also obviates the repeated solicitation of an organization for jobs by the different treatment agencies in the community. Finally, since the number of individuals hired by any one organization is not large, PACT/NADAP has embarked on analysis of a pooled experience of over 700 individuals hired by a number of organizations to identify more sharply, as a basis for expending this effort, those factors that make for the success or failure of ex-drug abusers on the job. Preliminary findings indicate that, if carefully selected on the basis of their skills and if ready for employment, former drug abusers prove to be no different than similar employees with no drug-abuse history with respect to job progress as measured by attendance, punctuality, job performance, promotions, and job retention.

Organizations cannot, in fact, avoid their responsibility to deal with problems of drug abuse. Federal regulations, augmented by recent court decisions, have now explicitly included drug abuse (as well as alcoholism) among the handicaps that must be accorded equal employment opportunities. Except for certain jobs involving significant risk to the safety of others, an organization's refusal to consider employing a person whose drug abuse is under control (even though he or she may still be under treatment) can lead to a claim of discrimination.

Abuse of medication

While the abuse of illegal and unauthorized drugs is a serious problem, an even greater cause for concern is the reliance on drugs as an antidote to such stress-related symptoms as anxiety, tension, insomnia, and pain. What I am referring to here is the indiscriminate overprescription and overuse of prescription and over-the-counter medications, often complicated by the concomitant use of alcohol.

This problem came dramatically to the nation's attention when it was revealed that former First Lady Betty Ford had entered the Naval Hospital's alcohol and drug rehabilitation center at Long Beach, California, for help in combating her "dependency on drugs." She had been using a combination of prescription drugs along with alcohol for her arthritis and chronic neck pain and, just as candidly as she had discussed her mastectomy in 1974, she explained that "over a period of time I got to the point where I was overmedicating myself. It's an insidious thing and I mean to rid myself of its damaging effects."

More recently, Jerry Lewis, the world-renowned comedian, announced that with medical help he had put an end to eight years of dependence on Percodan, a drug prescribed to relieve persistent pain from a back injury sustained when he twisted "the wrong way" in taking a pratfall in one of his performances. Originally, one tablet every few hours provided relief, but when the pain persisted, he found it necessary to use increasingly large amounts of the drug much more frequently in order to get through the day, even when he was not performing.

Some years ago, I was consulted by another famous stage actor who had developed a dual dependency. To overcome fatigue and to get himself "up" for the stress of the nightly performance, he took gradually increasing doses of amphetamines and other stimulants. Then, because these left him too "jazzed-up" to sleep, he would have several bedtime drinks accompanied by some sleeping pills instead of peanuts. This was known only to his wife, his manager, and the numerous doctors across the country who wrote the prescriptions that enabled him to maintain his supplies of these medications. It took many months of intensive treatment to wean him from these dependencies.

This tiny group of cases is atypical only in that men outnumber women. Actually, a recent study from the National Institute on Drug Abuse reports, there are about 20 million women in the United States with a drug-abuse and alcohol problem—more than twice the number of men (Nellis, 1977).

This is a difficult problem to combat in the work setting. Many stress reactions produce symptoms for which medication is quite appropriate, at least on a short-term basis during the acute phase. Pill taking is an intensely personal matter, particularly when it is legitimized by a physician's prescription. Overmedication and drug dependence, with or without alcohol abuse, are not easily identified in an employee population until they begin to interfere with individuals' work performance or produce changes in behavior and attitude. When this occurs, the individual should be referred for evaluation and appropriate treatment.

Certain preventive measures can be helpful. Perhaps the most useful is an educational program, ideally incorporated into a more comprehensive health promotion program (see pp. 187ff), that emphasizes the hazards of drug abuse. This should be accompanied by steps to limit the availability of medications on the premises. The overt pill popper, the person whose desk drawer contains a collection of assorted medicines that he or she generously shares, the office first aid cabinet that becomes a repository for psychoactive drugs available for the taking—these should be controlled as part of an effort to create a negative climate for self-medication.

Where there is an employee health unit, its policies and practices in relation to dispensing and prescribing medications should be examined as part of the periodic evaluation of its activities. For example, when I operated an employee health center, I made it a hard and fast rule never to dispense medications or provide prescriptions via messengers. No matter how exalted his or her title, no executive could send a secretary to pick up a few pills or a renewal prescription (frequently, the pills were for secretaries who use their bosses' names to avoid having to explain why they wanted them). Each individual had to appear in person so that I could satisfy myself that he or she needed them and was using them properly. With the individual's permission, contact was made with his or her personal physician to make sure that we were not being "whipsawed" into overprescribing. Needless to say, we constantly looked to the possibility of controlling or finding better ways to cope with the stressor that appeared to be responsible for the symptoms.

To summarize, drug abuse is a two-faceted problem: the use of illicit drugs and the vocational rehabilitation of individuals whose abuse and/or dependency have been brought under control; and the excessive and improper use of medications, often combined with alcohol, to relieve symptoms associated with stress reactions. Its solution lies in the promotion of understanding and attitudes that mitigate against drug abuse, training supervisory and managerial staff to recognize as early as possible the patterns of behavior and work performance that identify the individual in difficulty, and establishing in-house or in the community the professional resources to which such individuals may be referred for evaluation and proper treatment.

BACKACHE

Backache (low back pain) is an extremely common stress reaction that is particularly burdensome both to the employee and to the work organization. Its exact incidence is not known, but it has been said that 80 percent of the population will experience at least one disabling episode during adult life. Most backaches are attributed to an acute strain or trauma resulting from an attempt to lift something or an injudicious movement. Careful investigation, however, frequently reveals that the precipitating incident was coincidental, the real cause being chronic tension, stiffness, and weakness of key postural muscles induced by stress. Especially in sedentary individuals in whom these muscles are weakened by inactivity, the tension itself can produce a soreness but, more important, it also leaves the muscles vulnerable to injury by a sudden or strenuous movement.

Fortunately, most of these back episodes are mild; they generally respond to a week or two of rest and home remedies. Like the common cold, they are so common and the treatments so well known that most victims treat themselves without seeing a physician.

The physician becomes involved when the pain is unusually severe or persistent or when, because the cause of the initial episode has not been corrected, the episodes are recurrent. Unless the physician is aware of the key role of stress in the development of this disorder, the victim is started on what has been termed the "treatment treadmill." X rays are taken and, in 20 to 60 percent of cases, depending on how rigorously they are interpreted, they show structural defects or evidence of "arthritis" that have been associated with "instability" and pain in the spine (actually, they are found with similar frequency in individuals without pain). The patient is hospitalized for several weeks of traction and physical therapy, usually with a diagnosis of "disc disease." Consultations are arranged with orthopedists, neurologists, neurosurgeons, etc. Special X rays and diagnostic procedures are performed and nerve blocks and other kinds of injections may be tried. When these fail, surgery to correct the structural defect is usually advised.

The brochure describing the Spine Pain Program of the Memorial Hospital Medical Center in Long Beach, California, notes that: "when recovery does not progress normally, however, the problem can become chronic and, at its worst, catastrophic. Absences from work multiply or become prolonged. Repeated hospitalization and surgery may become more and more frequent. Marital and home life may deteriorate. Psychological and emotional conflicts as a result may become as severe as the physical problem." This program offers hospitalization for a complete diagnostic workup including evaluations by a team of different specialists followed by a comprehensive regimen of treatment that includes physical and occupational therapy, education, counseling, and weekly group discussions with psychologists and social workers.

Similar programs are offered by a number of medical centers in different parts of the country, but many patients are unable or unwilling to seek them out. Instead, they simply struggle along with more or less chronic discomfort and disability that generally fluctuate with the level of stress in their work or home life. They drift from doctor to doctor seeking a permanent cure. They buy braces, orthopedic supports, and home-treatment gadgets and take large amounts of pain relievers, tranquilizers, muscle relaxants, and other medications. When frustrated by physicians' inability or indifference, they turn to chiropractors, acupuncture, and even more questionable modes of treatment.

Data are not available on which accurate estimates of the cost of backache may be based. Backache was the fifth most common complaint responsible for a physician's office visit (sore throat ranked sixth, and cough, ninth) in the National Ambulatory Medical Care Survey of visits to office-based physicians in 1975 conducted by the National Center for Health Statistics (1977). Millions of dollars are spent each year on medications, orthopedic appliances, and gadgets designed to ease backache. Analysis of disability claims paid in 1976 by the Massachusetts Mutual Life Insurance Company revealed that back disorders accounted for 14.2 percent of claims and 17.7 percent of the benefits paid. Since most episodes can easily be attributed to some kind of incident during work, it is not surprising to find back problems looming large in workers' compensation statistics. Of the cases closed in 1973 by the New York Workers' Compensation Board, 18 percent involved back problems.

Thus, backache extracts a considerable toll in terms of an organization's expense for sickness and disability benefits as well as its workers' compensation experience. Nevertheless, such figures represent only the "tip of the iceberg." Not included is the impact on the countless individuals who needlessly become resigned to limitation of their activities and persistently recurrent discomfort.

The primary approach to this problem requires recognition of the fundamental role in its genesis played by stress and muscle deficiency and the opportunity to control those factors in the work setting that are inordinately stressful. But since stressors in their personal and home lives are equally if not more troublesome for most individuals, an approach is needed that will relieve their discomfort and increase their capacity to tolerate stress without initiating the back-pain syndrome. Such an approach is afforded by the "Y's Way to a Healthy Back Program" that was originally developed by Dr. Hans Kraus, the world-famous expert on back problems, and Alexander Melleby, Health and Physical Education Specialist at the West Side YMCA in New York City (Kraus, et al., 1977). It is now available in over 450 YMCA's across the country and abroad and, following a successful initial pilot project at the White Plains, New York, plant of the Long Lines Division of American Telephone and Telegraph, has been adopted as an in--house program by a number of industrial and governmental organizations.

The genesis of the Y program was a study by Dr. Kraus and his colleagues at the Columbia Presbyterian Medical Center of over 3,000 consecutive patients referred by physicians to a multidisciplinary back clinic. Over 80 percent showed no pathologic factors such as disc disease, arthritis, tumors, or injury to account for their back pain. However, each failed one or more of a battery of six simple tests of the strength and flexibility of key posture muscles (Kraus, 1970). This led to the development of an exercise program individualized to correct these particular muscular deficiencies, supplemented by relaxation training and limbering and stretching exercises. A large percentage of these patients were helped but when they stopped the exercises and returned to their sedentary existence, the tension-producing stressors of their work and sedentary urban lives soon led to a recurrence of their discomfort. Resumption of the exercise ritual usually brought renewed relief. Long-term follow-up of these individuals, and many others to whom the exercise routine was taught, demonstrated that adherence to the program led to disappearance of symptoms, freedom from recurrences, improved well-being, and a greater range of activity.

Because the number of back-pain victims is too large and the cost of treating them by physicians and back clinics too prohibitive, Dr. Kraus and Mr. Melleby designed and successfully tested a group program that would draw on the availability and accessibility of the YMCA's and their staffs of physical-fitness educators. These individuals were trained to perform the simple tests of minimal postural muscle fitness and to conduct the special exercise programs. They were also trained to identify individuals who should not enter the program or continue in it and guide them to obtain appropriate medical evaluation.

The program involves a group of no more than fifteen men and women who attend two one-hour sessions a week for six weeks. After taking the simple muscle-fitness tests, the exercises are demonstrated and taught in the sequence that is an essential part of the program: simple relaxation training, limbering and "warm-up" exercises, stretching exercises, muscle-strengthening exercises, and then, reversing the sequence, stretching exercises and "cooling off" exercises finishing with the relaxation training. An additional exercise is added at each session until the full sequence designed for the individual has been mastered.

Special facilities are not required, only a large enough room with a chair and a small, inexpensive exercise mat for each participant. The exercises are performed in everyday clothing and, since they are not strenuous, showers and changing rooms are not required.

Performance of the exercises once or twice a day at home is a key part of the program. Each participant is provided with an illustrated manual and a tape casette of recorded instructions. At the end of the six-week course, the participants are expected to continue the exercises indefinitely on their own.

The program has been completed at least once in more than 50 Y's and work organizations with essentially similar results: About one-third of the participants reported complete disappearance of all pain and the resumption of full activity; about one-third reported much less pain and some increase in range of activity; about one-quarter reported some improvement; and the remaining 10 percent were essentially unchanged. No significant adverse effects were encountered. It is still too early for the long-term follow-up that has been planned.

Although not part of its design, it has been observed that many participants in the program have used it as a springboard for other beneficial changes in life-style such as smoking cessation, better nutrition, weight control, and improved cardiovascular fitness (see p. 163). Although no systematic study has yet been performed, many participants reported greater ease in coping with the stress of their job.

As National Consultant to the program, Melleby has educated the YMCA regional physical education specialists and instructor-trainers to conduct instructor training courses for YMCA staff members and representatives of organizations interested in having their own programs. Special manuals for trainers and guidelines developed by the national YMCA staff and a medical advisory committee headed by Dr. Kraus provide the ongoing direction required to maintain the quality and integrity of the programs.

In summary, the "Y's Way to a Healthy Back Program" provides a readily available, quite inexpensive approach to the pervasive and costly problem of backache caused by stress and muscle deficiency.

MASS PSYCHOGENIC ILLNESS

Within a two-week period, thirty workers in an electronics asembly plant complained of such symptoms as headache, dizziness, lightheadedness, sleepiness, and nausea. The onset of symptoms was preceded by awareness of a strange odor, and they cleared gradually following rest at home.

Twenty-nine women in a plant assembling aluminum furniture, a nonmanufacturing process in which no chemicals are used, complained of headache, bad taste in the mouth, dry mouth, dizziness, and lightheadedness after smelling a strange odor. Several reported seeing a "blue mist" over one section of the plant. As word spread among the more than 300 workers in that plant, there was near panic and it was shut down. Air samples from the plant were analyzed but no toxic chemicals or other agents were detected. When the plant resumed operations several days later, twenty-seven employees, eight of whom had been involved in the initial outbreak, reported to the first-aid room with similar symptoms.

About one hour after starting work, thirty-five employees in a frozen-fish packing plant became ill complaining of headache, difficulty in breathing, dizziness, and weakness. Several years earlier there had been a carbon-monoxide exposure in that plant in which several of these workers had been affected. Although the symptoms were quite different, it was felt that this was probably the cause. However, a continuously recording carbon-monoxide detector that had been installed in the work area following the original exposure demonstrated that the amount of carbon monoxide in the air at the time of the outbreak had been far below the level at which any ill effects might be expected (Smith, et al., 1978).

These are three reported incidents of mass psychogenic illness, a phenomenon of the work setting that is currently attracting increasing interest and attention. Known also as "epidemic hysteria" and "assembly-line hysteria," it has been called "psychic possession" because of its similarity to outbreaks that were common all over Europe during the Middle Ages. In a factory in Southeast Asia, an epidemic did not subside until the manager hired a faith healer to drive away the "demons" to whom the native workers attributed their symptoms. The phenomenon has also been reported in schools and other closely knit communities. It is not new, having been noted and understood by more observant and sophisticated occupational physicians so often that it has led them to label emotional illness as a "miasma" of the workplace, a veritable contagion that can spread among the susceptible members of a group just like measles or chicken pox. Now that it has been dignified by a label, it is currently being studied by occupational health professionals and behavioral scientists in an effort to elucidate its causes and any particular characteristics that may make people more susceptible to it.

A group with the Behavioral and Motivational Factors Branch of the Motivation and Stress Research Section of the National Institute of Occupational Safety and Health has been particularly energetic. From their base at the Robert A. Taft Laboratories in Cincinnati, they have dispatched teams of physicians, psychologists, behavioral scientists, and industrial hygienists to plants and factories in response to calls for help from federal, state, and local investigators who had not been able to find the cause of an outbreak of illness. They have visited shoe and electronics factories, a fish-packing plant, a lawn furniture firm, and others, and have concluded that the actual incidence of mass psychogenic illness is much higher than has been reported in the medical literature.

On the basis of their painstaking study of the workers involved in these outbreaks and reports of similar investigations of other incidents, the NIOSH team developed the following profile of the typical affected worker:

> . . . a female, less educated than her peers, who works under great pressure to maintain a job to support her family. Poor relations with supervisors, role ambiguity, work overload, and the use of inferior materials are daily stressors. More importantly, opportunities for expressing ideas, grievances, or alleviation of difficulties are stymied so that the worker is without control over her

work-life, without pride or self-esteem. Having been left with no resource to cope with the situation, an objective physical stressor, such as the smell of a gas leak, can serve to provide justification to display somatic symptoms severe enough to necessitate a physician's care.

(COHEN ET AL., 1978)

Although a variety of symptoms has been reported, including skin rashes, abdominal pain, and vaginal discharge, they usually form a pattern characteristic of the "hyperventilation syndrome." This can be produced voluntarily—indeed, it has frequently been used as 'a "stunt" in hazing—by breathing in and out as rapidly as possible. This blows off the carbon dioxide produced by the body's metabolism to the point at which changes in the chemical balance of the blood occur. These lead to the characteristic symptoms: lightheadedness, dizziness, headache, tingling and numbness in the hands and feet, dryness of the mouth, a sense of anxiety, and, ultimately, fainting. In the faint, breathing slows and, as the carbon dioxide in the blood gradually returns to its normal level, the victim awakens, no worse for the wear.

In real life, the hyperventilation syndrome is a frightening experience. Although it is experienced by both sexes, it seems to occur more commonly among women. Its victims are characteristically people under chronic stress who are subject to moments of acute anxiety that may be spontaneous but more often are triggered by some external stimulus. For example, it is seen frequently in people with phobias who cannot avoid the situation in which they become fearful; such as the claustrophobic person who must ride a crowded elevator. The onset is usually a sudden sense of difficulty in breathing expressed as "not enough air," "a tight band around my chest," or "being suffocated." Breathing becomes shallow and rapid and, in a few moments, the other symptoms begin to appear. Abetted by the feeling of a "sense of impending disaster," they conjure up visions of having a heart attack or a stroke. Now, with a more "rational" basis for the fear, the anxiety increases and the full-blown syndrome emerges.

The victim's obvious distress attracts the attention of nearby people who gather around and try to help by loosening the individual's collar and belt, offering a drink, opening windows, etc. It seems quite certain that some deaths recorded as suicides occurred when an unsteady hyperventilating individual pitched out of the open window at which he or she was gasping for "more air." The symptoms gradually subside (they clear rapidly when the victim or someone nearby has been trained to abort the episode by placing an ordinary paper bag or some other receptacle over the nose and mouth so that the victim rebreathes the carbon dioxide that he or she is blowing off), leaving the individual exhausted, weak, and concerned about the portent of the incident.

When seen by a physician, especially one who had not previously seen the individual, and the full story does not emerge, either because the right questions are not asked or the patient is unable to suppy the answers at the time, an investigation is usually ordered. This also happens when the syndrome is recognized but the physician wants to make sure that it was not associated with something more serious. Electrocardiograms, blood tests, skull X rays, brain scans, and even spinal taps are frequently performed—often during several days in a hospital for "observation"—and if coincidental abnormalities or even equivocal findings are reported, the patient may be branded with the diagnosis of a serious organic disease which he or she does not have.

The implications to individuals are obvious. To their employers, it means a spell of absence and the needless drain of thousands of dollars on the group health-insurance benefits.

When it occurs in the workplace, the sight of one individual becoming ill because of a strange odor or some other real or fancied environmental stimulus can cause others to display similar symptoms. The news spreads quickly through the plant, producing mounting anxiety and confusion and, when more workers become ill, near panic may ensue. With the publicity given to the growing number of incidents of *bona fide* illness produced by exposures to chemicals and other potentially toxic agents, and employees who are dissatisfied with their working conditions and feeling put-upon by the employer, it is not surprising that something in the workplace is blamed for the outbreak.

This sets in motion a whole chain events. The employer initiates an investigation, using outside consultants when the organization lacks adequate expertise. Local, state, and federal health authorities to whom these outbreaks are invariably reported send in their own teams of environmental specialists. When nothing is found, the outbreak remains an unsolved mystery. But, sometimes small amounts of agents known to be capable of toxicity are found. Even though the amounts found are well below the minimum levels of the dangerous range established by safety standards and the symptoms are quite different from those ordinarily produced by the suspected toxin, suspicion is aroused that the standards were set too high and that the agent may really be the cause. Continuous monitoring is usually initiated to rule out the possibility that higher exposures may actually have occurred and changes in materials, equipment, and processes may be ordered to eliminate the toxin from the workplace or to reduce it to an even lower level. The presumed association of the outbreak with the suspected toxin may be cited repeatedly until it is regarded as fact and used as an argument to promote the promulgation of new, more stringent standards that may be needlessly costly or impossible for industry to obey.

All of this takes time, during which operations are halted or impeded, and the organization, and sometimes the industry of which it is a part, is under a cloud. The chain of increasingly detailed investigations is costly as are the engineering and other changes in the work process required for more effective environmental controls. The involved workers or their representatives may institute worker compensation, negligence, or product liability claims which, even when not successful, are costly to defend. Most important of all, all of this constitutes a giant smoke screen in which the real cause of the outbreak is hidden and which prevents the implementation of appropriate corrective measures.

While the distinctive pattern of mass psychogenic illness is easy to recognize when it is full blown, it often develops gradually rather than in the kind of explosive outbreaks described by the NIOSH investigators. As our knowledge of toxic occupational exposures grows, we find increasing evidence that doses much smaller than those that cause outright poisoning may have very subtle effects. Also, there are literally thousands of chemicals in use, to say nothing of the infinite variety of chemical combinations, whose toxicity has not been exhaustively studied. Accordingly, it would be prudent to investigate the work premises sufficiently to be reasonably certain that an environmental exposure is not at fault. But once that is done—or better, while it is going on, for it is possible to have a dual causation—the spotlight should be focused on the stressors arising from the work, the working conditions, and the relationships among the workers, their supervisors, and the organization. Employees will be reassured by the correction of physical deficiencies in the workplace disclosed by the investigation, even if they are remotely or not at all related to the outbreak. These are things that should be done anyway, such as improving exhaust ventilation, silencing noisy machinery, and reducing glare. The real solution, however, will come from measures, described elsewhere in this book, that will identify and control the work-related sources of stress.

ABSENTEEISM

Generally recognized as the major cause of lost productivity, sick absence (i.e., absence attributed to sickness) is one of the primary indicators of stress within an organization. It is a universal problem which seems to be increasing throughout the industrialized world, and organizations everywhere are seeking better ways to control it.

Most organizations have a dual attitude toward sick absence. On the one hand, they appreciate that people do become ill and unable to work. This is reflected in increasingly generous policies of paid sick leave and other benefits to ease the burden that illness places on the employee. Organizations perceive that when some employees are not quite well they may recover more rapidly if they take time off for rest and proper treatment. In fact, such individuals can actually be a liability on the job when they present a burden to supervisors and coworkers who must compensate for their impaired functional capacity and when they may be responsible for costly errors and accidents.

On the other hand, organizations are plagued by losses attributable to what they regard as unnecessary and needlessly prolonged sick absences. They are aware that many voluntary absences are attributed to sickness because it is an easier and more acceptable explanation.* Also, they recognize that in many instances slightly incapacitated employees could continue to perform adequately without risk to themselves or their coworkers if they were motivated to stay on the job.

Discussions of sick absence seem to polarize these attitudes and lead managers and employee representatives to make simplistic pronouncements that reveal their frustrations and their prejudices. For

---

* Working mothers traditionally report themselves ill when they have to stay home to look after a sick child or other family member while their husbands, whose careers are considered more important, continue to work. Among uniformed municipal employees, such as the police and firefighters, who frequently are allowed unlimited sick leave with full pay while their wives have jobs where paid sick leave is limited, it is the husband who reports ill and stays home to tend the sick child.

example, it is said that "people stay away from work for one of two reasons—either they are prevented from attending, or they choose not to attend." Union leaders bargain for increasingly liberal benefits while managers grumble, "cut sick-pay allowances and absences will drop." Complaints are voiced such as, "the main cause of sick absence is malingering," and "doctors will certify anything as a 'legitimate' illness." Managers propose get-tough, punitive systems based on home visits to make sure that the absent employee is really sick enough to be confined or hospitalized and is receiving professional attention. Union leaders protest these as intrusive invasions of the employee's privacy and threaten to file grievances claiming that such enforcement procedures are "unreasonable." The observation that attendance records frequently improve when a work force faces reduction prompts the suggestion that "another million unemployed will cure the problem."

At the outset, it must be recognized that sick absence cannot be entirely eliminated. People will become ill and demonstrate objective evidence of incapacity that, by any reasonable set of standards, makes it impossible or inadvisable to work. Such evidence may be lacking in many cases of *bona fide* illness: short-term illnesses in which the signs are evanescent although the symptoms may persist a while longer; long-term illnesses or flare-ups of chronic disorders with no significant change in previously observed findings; and emotional illness and other disorders manifested only by attitudes and behavior whose incapacitating effects can only be inferred.

Such "real" illness accounts for only a portion of total sick absence. Because of varying definitions and criteria, there are no accurate statistics; I would estimate it to range around 40 percent. Even this portion, however, is significantly influenced by occupational stress. The contribution of stress to the genesis of chronic disorders such as coronary heart disease, hypertension, and peptic ulcer has been mentioned frequently. Every health professional working in industry has observed instances in which job stress has appeared to precipitate such acute episodes of illness as heart attacks, bouts of asthma, and bleeding ulcers, and every discerning practitioner has noted cases in which the patient's negative attitude to the job and its stressors has prolonged or compromised his or her recovery. Work stressors and the ability to modify them are often a critical determinant in planning return to work and on-the-job rehabilitation.

Malingering accounts for a very small portion of total sick absence. Much of it is found among employees who have come to regard the availability of a fixed amount of sick leave per year as paid "holidays" to which they are entitled. When the policy prohibits their carry-over and accumulation, there is usually an epidemic of "illness" toward the year end that uses up any residue of paid days. Although by no means limited to them, this kind of behavior is most frequently displayed by school teachers and other groups of civil service workers.

To discourage such malingering, a number of organizations have instituted the practice of allocating all or a portion of the salary costs of unused sick leave to a special fund that is distributed to employees as a cash bonus or used for employee recreation programs or work-place amenities that would not ordinarily be provided. Variations on this theme include awards for perfect attendance such as premium stamps, free dinners, extra vacation pay, and the temporary use of preferred parking places.

Such arrangements are frequently proposed by management consultants but, although they often produce an initial improvement, their costs often equal or exceed the savings as the absence rates gradually return to their earlier levels. In one organization, for example, a management which had proudly reported the success of a bonus program in reducing paid sick leave was chagrined when it was pointed out that the number of days of paid leave attributed to work-related injuries had gradually risen an equivalent amount. These were charged to worker compensation experience (most group insurance is "experience rated"; i.e., premium costs reflect the number and costs of the claims and their administration) and tabulated under another budget category that was not under the same scrutiny. In this instance, the employees enjoyed the same amount of paid sick leave *and* the bonuses while the organization was paying not only the bonuses and the costs of the program, but also those reflecting the worsening worker compensaton experience.

"True" malingering in the sense of consciously feigning the signs and symptoms of illness is not very common. At most, in my experience, it accounts for less than 1 percent of total absence. Malingerers are usually easy to identify—they tend to exhibit a consistent pattern of repeated absences and alleged illnesses and their lack of responsibility to their jobs permeates their behavior even when they are present. Handling them is essentially a managerial and supervisory function rather than a health matter, but it should be noted that, once in a while, even malingerers do become ill or injured.

The great bulk of sick absence is attributable to what has been called "sick behavior." This has a dual connotation. It reflects minor illness and partial incapacity in individuals with impaired motivation to work. It also includes symptoms that are functional in origin; that is, they are not caused by infection, trauma, or organic pathology, but by stress-induced functional aberrations. The symptoms are no less "real" than those of organic disease—although there may be exaggerated susceptibility to them—and they generally respond just as well to medication and conventional treatment. This is important to understand. There is an all-too-common pejorative attitude that such symptoms are "imaginary" and readily controlled by the appropriate exercise of "willpower."

Sick behavior varies with the nature of the illness and is modified by social, cultural, and personal factors. Thus, in any organization, a particular pattern of work stressors will produce varying types of sick behavior among different subsets of the employee population. The basic components of sick behavior are:

1   The individual is not responsible for the condition.

2   While sick, the individual is not expected to perform all of his or her normal activities.

3   The individual wants to get well.

4   The individual seeks technically competent professional help and submits rather passively to whatever may be offered in the way of treatment.

5   The individual usually does improve, but after a time or when the same levels of stress recur, the pattern recycles.

If this is understood, one can readily understand why sick behavior is so prevalent, why it tends to be repetitive, and why it is unlikely to respond to discipline or to conventional symptom-focused medical treatment. It also explains why absence-control programs that do not address it rarely produce more than transitory results. By the same token, it must be emphasized that any absence-control program that focuses only on sick behavior is not only likely to be similarly unsuccessful but will, in the long run, tend to legitimize its victims' passivity and dependency and may even encourage its prevalence. A proper absence-control program requires the coordinated application of multiple approaches by different people with sufficient flexibility to allow modifications that meet the needs of people with different social and cultural backgrounds, from different kinds of work situations, and at different times. Also it must recognize that, even though work stressors may play a role, the basic cause usually lies in stress arising intrinsically in an individual's personality or which the individual encounters away from work, in the family or in the community.

The *sine qua non* of an effective absence-control program is a record system that tabulates the number, timing, and frequency of sick absences and demonstrates the patterns exhibited by individuals and groups. Data from many different organizations in different parts of the world generally reveal that about 5 percent of the work force accounts for about one-third of the number of spells of absence, while another 5 percent accounts for about a third of the lost days. As a rule, these two small groups consist of different people. Younger people are generally responsible for the more frequent absences, while older employees who more frequently have serious health problems and multiple diseases are generally responsible for absences of longer duration.

A consistent finding is a small number of people who are never absent. They are not always the healthiest people; indeed, their routine medical examinations frequently disclose impairments and chronic disorders no less severe than those found in absentees. Although a number of studies have attempted to isolate their special characteristics, we cannot yet identify these individuals before they make such a record. Although many are found in management, a large number are found among the blue-collar rank-and-file workers whose motivation to work is not expected to be so high. They are not necessarily the best workers nor the most ambitious. Nor are they the most insecure with respect to holding on to their jobs. Perhaps the single common characteristic is their justifiable pride in their singular accomplishment. It is entirely appropriate to honor them for this achievement. It may even be useful to hold them out as examples to be emulated by their co-workers, but it must be acknowledged that they are fundamentally a rare and special breed.

Study of absence records yields another clue to effective absence control: The patterns of absence displayed during the first six months or year on the job tend to persist throughout the term of employment. This suggests that inquiry about one's absence record in his or her previous job may be a more reliable predictor of a job applicant's future attendance than the findings revealed by a preemployment medical examination. It also points to the desirability of initiating some kind of remedial effort early in the course of an individual's employment rather than attributing a faulty attendance record to "adjustment" problems that will "work themselves out" as the individual settles in the new job. Finally, it points out the value of a probation period during which an employee's response to that intervention can be tested before a "permanent" job commitment is made.

The now-classic studies conducted by Dr. Lawrence E. Hinkle, Jr., and Dr. Norman N. Plummer among the employees of the New York Telephone Company shortly after World War II emphasized that about one-third of the work force accounted for almost all of the absences due to serious illness. Of particular interest was their finding of clusters of illnesses that represented a significant departure from these employees' earlier more normal attendance record. These clusters, which spanned periods as long as five or ten years, generally comprised a series of illnesses that often were apparently totally unrelated. The common denominator, it seemed, was that at least the initial episode, and often many of the subsequent bouts, appeared to be related to a period of unusual stress. This was usually personal rather than work-related (these were generally well-established employees and, in those days at least, working conditions in the telephone company were quite stable).

The second essential of our prototype absence-control program is recognition that such programs are fundamentally the responsibility of line management. This means that management must set the rules and establish a fair but firm set of disciplinary procedures to enforce them. By allowing workers a voice in establishing those rules and procedures through their unions or elected representatives, they are more likely to be acceptable.

The primary responsibility for administering the program is delegated to first-line supervisors. But it takes more than simply handing them a set of printed procedures to follow. They must be trained, either as a separate exercise or as part of a more comprehensive supervisor training program. This should involve indoctrination in the necessity and rationale of the program and schooling in the various steps the procedures may require them to take. Demonstrations or, better still, role-playing exercises in applying them to different kinds of employees are usually valuable tools. In my experience, more than one well-conceived absence-control program has failed because of inadequate supervisor training and performance.

Incidentally, once the program is under way, a pattern of increasing absence in a work unit or one that varies from those of comparable groups in the organization may suggest that the group is experiencing an increased level of work stress or it may point to a problem of the supervisor to which the employees are reacting.

In one organization, for example, quarterly budget reports indicated an increase in expenditures for paid absence. This was first noted in the report for the second quarter; by the third, it had climbed to the amount budgeted for the full year. This trend was out of phase with the usual seasonal fluctuations in absences and there had been no epidemics of illness in the community that might explain it. Analysis of absence data indicated that the increase was being produced by upper-level technical workers and their supervisors in two divisions of the organization. For the most part, these were ambitious young to middle-aged employees with highly marketable skills in departments that had been the subject of much gossip. It was known that outside consultants had been studying their activities and it was rumored that these units would be scattered around the country as part of a regionalization program or, even worse, that they would be abolished with their functions being performed under a contract with an independent service organization. While most of the sick absence was attributed to stress-induced symptoms, a rise in resignations made it apparent that a good part of it had been devoted to job-hunting.

In many programs, verification and certification procedures are used to identify instances of abuse and malingering. In one organization, supervisory-level personnel are required to telephone one or more times a day to the homes of employees who have reported themselves sick to confirm that they are really ill at home rather than out moonlighting or at a ball game. Another organization employs a staff of part-time physicians whose chief duty appears to be visits to the homes of all absent employees and, when necessary, performing a physical examination to substantiate the reported illness. Such verification procedures are often not inexpensive and, in my view, except when launching a new disciplinary process in a work force with well-entrenched patterns of absence abuse, are rarely cost effective, especially when applied to every absence. In some organizations in which they formerly were routine, they are now being reserved for selected cases in which absence abuse is strongly suspected.

Absence certification is another procedure of similarly question-able value when applied routinely to all absences. It requires that when absent employees return to work they must provide a statement by their personal physicians certifying that they had been ill and are now well enough to resume their usual activities. Without such a statement, the absence is considered "unexcused' which means that the employee will not be paid for that period and may be a target for disci-plinary action.

In some organizations, absentees must report to the employee health unit for "clearance" before being allowed to return to work. Such clearance procedures are valid for workers in jobs demanding high levels of performance, such as airline pilots, steeplejacks, and nurses in acute care units. They are also valid when it is suspected that employees may be placing themselves and their coworkers at risk by trying to return to work too soon, when there is concern about the employee's ability to obtain needed medical attention, and when invoked early and at repeated intervals during a long absence to con-firm that proper attention is being paid to reconditioning and rehabili-tation programs that will shorten the absence and reduce any residual impairment.

However, their value is questionable when used routinely as a means of controlling absence abuse. They make wardens out of physi-cians, a role in which they are usually not comfortable, particularly when they are expected to deny their patients' wishes and expecta-tions. Further, especially in short illnesses, the signs may have com-pletely cleared and physicians are simply certifying what the employees told them. In fact, some physicians refuse to see patients for this purpose, having a nurse or office clerk sign their names to the forms that their patients are required to produce. I even know one physician who hands such patients a preprinted signed form allowing them to write in the applicable dates and the nature of the illness. One organization requires absent employees to visit the office of one of a network of physicians paid to provide such clearances. Investigation revealed not only that the reliability of these clearances was question-able, but that absences were actually prolonged because it frequently took an extra day or two for the employee to get an appointment with the certifying doctor.

Most organizations are unaware of a hidden cost when employees are required to be certified by a personal physician for short-term absences: the impact of these "ceremonial" physician visits on the organization's health-insurance experience. Many organizations have become quite concerned about the rapidly rising cost of their health-insurance premiums. One approach to their containment has been an effort to reduce the needless utilization of health services. While this has focused primarily on hospital care, a number of organizations have launched campaigns to cut down on "unnecessary" physicians' visits, a feature of which has been the promotion of self-care for common minor ailments for which the physician can usually offer very little. Yet one of these organizations has been undercutting this effort by continuing to require a medical certification when such illnesses lead to absences from work.

The major thrust of the absence-control program picks up where these disciplinary measures leave off. Individuals with long or repeated absences, especially those of a single day attached to a weekend, are identified and referred to trained counselors (social workers and nurses are ideal candidates for this activity) for investigation of the causes of their absences. Often the problem is found to be "real" and already being adequately addressed. It frequently turns out to be a problem within the family; in such instances, the counselor assists the employee to contact the most appropriate resources for help to resolve it. When, as is often the case, the problem is sick behavior, the counselor refers the individual to treatment in the organization's stress-management program or to prearranged outside resources. At the same time, the counselor evaluates any work-related stressors that may be involved to see if they can be reduced to more tolerable levels until the employee's capacity to cope with them is improved.

Even when pursued in ideal fashion, such a program will not solve all absence problems. Those in which it fails call for special action, such as a complete change of job to one that might be better tolerated or separation of the individual from the organization. It is a mistake to continue to employ such individuals: It not only perpetuates their difficulty, but, sooner or later, it undermines the whole absence-control program.

To summarize, excessive or abnormal patterns of absenteeism are frequently a symptom of stress. When presented by individuals they generally represent personal difficulties compounded by stressors arising in the work situation. When presented by groups, they usually indicate an organizational problem. Absence control is fundamentally a disciplinary matter based on an adequate record-keeping system. To be effective, however, the discipline should be augmented by stress-management programs to which chronic absentees can be referred for identification and control of the stressors that may be causing the difficulty.

REFERENCES

Armor, D. J.; J. M. Polic; and H. B. Stanbul (1976). *Alcoholism and Treatment*. Santa Monica, Cal.: The Rand Corporation, R-1739-NIAAA.

Cloud, L. A. (1974). "Treatment is not the problem." *Labor-Management Alcoholism Journal* 4:22–23.

Cohen, B. G. F.; M. J. Colligan; W. Wester; and M. J. Smith (1978). An investigation of job satisfaction factors in an incident of Mass Psychogenic Illness at the workplace. *Occup. Health Nursing* 26:10–16.

Faler, P. (1974). Cultural aspects of the industrial revolution: Lynn, Massachusetts shoemakers and industrial morality, 1826–1860. *Labor History* 15:367–394.

Jankowaski, C., and D. E. Drum (Nov. 1977). Criteria for the diagnosis of alcoholism. *Arch. Int. Med* 137:1532–1536.

Kraus, H. (1970). *Clinical Treatment of Back and Neck Pain*. New York: McGraw Hill.

Kraus, H.; A. Melleby; and R. R. Gaston (July 1977). Back pain correction and prevention. *N. Y. State Journal of Medicine* 77:1335–1338.

Mulford, H. A. (Sept. 1977). Women and men problem drinkers. *J. Studies of Alcohol* 138:1624–1639.

National Center for Health Statistics (1977). *Ambulatory Medical Care Rendered in Physicians' Offices: U.S. 1975*. Hyattsville, Md.; Advance Data No. 12.

Nellis, M. (1977). *Drugs, Alcohol and Women's Health*. Bethesda, Md.: National Institute on Drug Abuse.

Noble, E. P., ed. (June 1978). *Third Special Report to the U.S. Congress on Alcohol and Health from the Secretary of Health, Education and Welfare*. Rockville, Md.: National Institute on Alcohol Abuse and Alcoholism.

Pessen, E. (1978). Builders of the young republic. In R. B. Morris (ed.), *The American Worker*. Washington, D.C.: U.S. Dept. of Labor, pp. 70–71.

Smith, M. J.; M. J. Colligan; and J. J. Hurrell (June 1978). Three incidents of industrial mass psychogenic illness. *J. Occup. Med.* 20:399–400.

10

CHANGE
AS A STRESSOR

In this chapter I want to present the concept of change itself as a stressor. In the workplace, the changes that are the most pervasive include the frequent changes associated with shift work and the more sweeping changes involved in relocation; the changes in the work force associated with the new roles of women; the changes in individuals that we call the "mid-life" crisis; and the ultimate change, retirement.

SHIFT WORK

Shift work (work hours outside of the conventional daytime range) is increasing as more industries seek to maximize the operation of expensive capital equipment. Formerly, continuous operation was limited to industries dependent on equipment or chemical reactions that cannot be started and completed on a single shift. Steel mills, oil refineries, and large chemical plants are typical examples of these industries. Today, however, it is becoming increasingly prevalent in white-collar industries, thanks largely to the introduction of data-processing equipment. Continuous operation is dictated not only by the need to amortize the high cost of computers and accessory equipment, but by the need for rapid turn-around in the processing of information.

There are also the traditional round-the-clock industries which provide services that are needed twenty-four hours a day. Typical examples include hospitals, police and fire departments, public transportation, public utilities, and the whole gamut of industries serving the public's "off-hours" requirements, such as restaurants, night clubs, hotels, and cleaning services.

A recent survey conducted by the National Institute of Occupational Safety and Health indicates that there are many types of shift schedules and patterns of rotation. For example, the International Association of Fire Fighters reported about 150 different types of work schedules for firefighters alone. Although available sources did not provide precise data, it would appear that, in this country, about 5 million workers are engaged in shift work with the largest numbers as well as proportions being found in the food-processing, transportation, and health-care industries (Tasto and Colliger, 1977).

In Sweden, about one-third of all employees (some 1.2 million) work what they call "uncomfortable" hours. It is not surprising, therefore, that the impact of shift work on health and well-being has been a major focus at the Laboratory for Clinical Stress Research at the Karolinska Institutet in Stockholm where, under the direction of Dr. Lennart Levi, Professor of Psychosocial Environmental Medicine, many studies of shift workers have been undertaken. One of the earliest, a questionnaire study of several hundred shift workers, showed them to have higher frequencies of sleep, mood, digestive, and social disturbances than workers on the day shift (Levi, 1978).

In another study, Dr. Levi and his associates studied the physiological, psychological, and social reactions in habitual daytime workers who were transferred to the night shift for a three-week period. They found that although the endocrine system did adapt to the change by "stepping on the gas" to keep awake at night and "slowing down" during the day to allow for some sleep, the basic biologic rhythms had not fully adapted by the end of the three-week period. In addition, they found that the three-week switch from habitual day work to the night shift was accompanied by increases in a number of the indices of physiologic stress and social problems in the workers and in their families (Levi, 1978).

Such research is part of the newly developed science of chronobiology, the study of the rhythms that all living organisms display. It is not yet known whether these are intrinsic characteristics of living cells or responses to such external natural rhythms as the day-night cycle, phases of the moon, and seasons of the year. However, as we learn more about them, it becomes apparent that they influence virtually every body function and underlie many of the social patterns to which we have become accustomed. Knowledge of their pervasiveness and of the effects of their disruption is important information for those in jobs that must be performed around the clock and those who embark on prolonged missions in space, beneath the sea, in subterranean caves, or in polar regions where diurnal changes in lighting, sunshine, and social activities, especially feeding and sleeping times, deviate from the norm. It is also important to the manager contemplating relocation of a plant or trying to coordinate the activities of plants in widely separated geographic locations.

Short-term or "ultradian" rhythms recycle every 90 to 100 minutes. Best known of these are the rapid eye movement (REM) periods of sleep which signal the onset of the 90-minute sleep cycles. Disruption of these sleep cycles has been shown to be associated with nightmares and loss of the restorative benefits of sleep. Such waking phenomena as hunger pangs, fluctuations in sleepiness, alertness, and daydreaming have also been shown to have 90-minute swings throughout the day. This suggests that mid-morning and mid-afternoon coffee breaks really do have some rationale.

The "circadian," or twenty-four-hour, cycles are probably the most extensively studied in animals as well as humans and have been given the appellation of "biological clocks." They are displayed by measurements of the adrenal and pituitary hormones that mediate the body's response to stress, insulin and other hormone systems, heart rate, blood pressure, and body temperature. The last is perhaps the most basic body indicator since it reflects the sum total of energy production and loss of energy. These cycles are also displayed by sensory acuity, ability to solve problems, eye-to-hand coordination, and mood.

Desynchronization of these circadian rhythms is produced by shift changes and by travel between time zones. It has been associated with a wide variety of physiologic and performance parameters. In a large metropolitan newspaper whose pressworkers rotated shifts every month, for example, the accident rates peaked on the first tour of the new shift.

The "jet lag" experienced by people who travel rapidly across time zones usually reflects the desynchronization of biologic clocks rather than travel fatigue. This has been universally recognized as the reason for the poor results so often achieved by business representatives and diplomats who rush into important meetings and negotiating sessions soon after a long east-west or west-east plane flight. To counter this, many organizations require their representatives to schedule at least a day of rest before conducting any business at the end of such flights.

Interestingly, although human circadian rhythms have a day-night cycle, they do not always coincide with sunrise and sunset. This variability accounts for the "larks," the "day people," who are already in high gear when the alarm goes off and tend to run down in late afternoon and early evening, and for the "owls," the "night people," who take as long as three to four hours to get going in the morning and seem to gather energy and momentum as the day goes on. Experiments at the Chronobiology Laboratories at the University of Minnesota show that each person has his or her own set of biologic rhythms. (Note: These are not to be confused with the three invariable "biorhythm cycles," described on pp. 173ff, which chronobiologists regard as "unscientific bunk.") They are now being studied in relation to the timing of doses of medication on the theory that, if cancer cells show a fluctuation in metabolism, it may be possible to time doses of chemotherapeutic agents so that they will have a maximal effect on the tumor with less likelihood of causing the distressing side effects. Other studies suggest that an asynchrony in biologic rhythms may be responsible for aberrations in mood and behavior displayed by manic-depressives and that these may be controlled by getting these rhythms back "in tune."

Seasonal variations are generally associated with changes in climate. Hot, humid weather, for example, is usually associated with fatigue, lassitude, low creativity, and a propensity for making errors. It is interesting that acts of violence and riots occur most commonly during the warm season and that the monthly suicide rates in European countries invariably peak during the summer.

Long spells of rigorous cold weather seem to produce irritability and depression. "Cabin fever" was the term applied to this syndrome among prospectors and homesteaders in the Far West and Alaska around the turn of the century. Now somewhat milder because the weather-enforced confinement and isolation can be overcome, this syndrome is still seen toward the end of the long winter in the North Central states and Canada and is probably responsible for the popularity of late winter and early spring vacations among people working in these regions.

Finally, there are seasonal meterologic phenomena such as the hot winds common to many areas around the world known by such names as the Fohn in Germany, the Sirocco in Italy, Chamssin or Sharau in Israel, Chinook in Canada, Santa Anna in Southern California, and the Northern Winds in Australia. These cause a wide range of psychological and physical disturbances in which a similar pattern seems to emerge: headache, irritability, changes in mood, predisposition to accidents, and a greater frequency of heart attacks and strokes.

Much work needs to be done to truly understand all these biologic rhythms, but it seems quite clear that they are associated with a wide range of physiologic and psychologic alterations that significantly affect work capacities, creativity, and interpersonal relationships. It is evident that in structuring jobs, planning work assignments, and initiating changes such as plant relocation, managers who understand them and know what it takes to adjust to their desynchronization will achieve better results.

Shift work is highly prized by many employees. Some enjoy the pay premiums it frequently provides; for others, it provides the opportunity to pursue hobbies that would be thwarted by regular hours. Off-hour work enables some employees to look after their children and meet other family responsibilities.

On the other hand, shift work is not well tolerated by individuals with such chronic diseases as diabetes, arthritis, and hypertension. Pregnant women often have difficulty adjusting to shift changes and may have to take an earlier, more prolonged maternity leave if it is not possible to arrange to have regular hours.

Most of the stress of shift work comes from being out of step with the rest of the community. Shift workers often have difficulty sleeping and fitting family, social, and recreational activities into their schedules. Some organizations have made special efforts to ease some of these problems. These include special commuting arrangements to make up for unsatisfactory public transportation, shopping services, and special recreational programs. In several organizations, high-level managers make a particular point of scheduling regular visits to the workplace during evening and night shifts to convey by their presence their awareness that the shift workers are no less an important part of the organization than those they encounter during the "normal" working hours.

RELOCATION

The mobility of Americans is legendary. Census maps show marked shifts in population from urban centers to suburbia to exurbia, from the Northeast and North Central areas to the "Sun Belt" regions of the South and West. Industry moves its plants or builds new ones in response to such attractions as tax concessions, lower energy costs, and a more favorable labor market. These moves generate in turn the migration of the organizations and people who provide essential services, ranging from utilities, department stores, and supermarkets to small retail shops and tradespeople. People are moving too, to seek new careers, to find new climates and social environments, to join or get away from relatives and friends.

These migrations present stressors and cause problems, but this section will examine only those that involve employees whose moves are dictated by reassignment within their organizations. They are mostly on the middle-management levels with the skills and experience required to direct the operation of a new unit, plant, or facility, or one that has been acquired by the organization. Many in formal management-training programs or who are climbing the promotion ladder are relocated not only to fill a job but to provide them with diversified experience and new challenges to overcome. For these people frequent relocation becomes an integral part of a successful career path. In the Northwestern Bell Telephone Company, for example, a manager might be moved fifteen times or more before reaching his or her final position, and in I.B.M. the company logo has been said to mean, "I'm being moved!" According to a survey, the nation's 600 largest companies transferred almost 100,000 employees during 1976. To these must be added an equal number who, it is estimated, were moved by smaller companies not reached by the survey. These figures represent an increase of about 10 percent over the previous year.

Relocation represents a considerable investment by the organization. Exact figures are not available but, even if they were, they would probably not indicate the toll extracted by the stressors with which the employees and their families are burdened. Nor would they include the cost to the organization when the move doesn't work out and the employees have to be recalled or replaced. This often sets in motion a sequence of additional transfers as the organization scrambles to cover the situation.

Most organizations have a relocation program that provides their employees with financial benefits and help in making the move. Some have staff persons assigned to provide such help, but most turn to the growing number of firms providing "relocation services." For a fee paid by the organization, these firms appraise the value of the employee's home and provide guidance in placing it on the market. Occasionally, they will buy it directly at a fair price or, if the employee does not wish to sell it, help to rent it and even manage the property until the employee is able to return to it. These firms provide information about the new area and introduce the employees to neighborhoods that meet their specifications and desires. They put employees in touch with responsible brokers and help them not only to find mortgage money for a new home but to get a loan to cover the down payment if the proceeds of the sale of the old home have not yet been realized. Finally, they provide assistance with the actual move, making the arrangements with a van line and advising what possessions to take and how they should be shipped.

The relocation benefits provided by the organization are often generous. They include guarantees against any loss of equity should the new house have to be sold later in a depressed real-estate market and reimbursement of closing costs, interest on the loan for the down payment, and any mortgage-rate differentials. They cover the costs of moving, reinstalling or replacing household appliances, carpets, and fixtures, and the expense of temporary quarters for the employee and the employee's family until the new home is ready for occupancy. They reimburse expenses involved in scouting trips by the employee and family to the new area, and the employee's back-and-forth travel on weekends until the family can be reunited in the new location.

These programs are indeed generous but, in my view, they are far from satisfactory. They address only the impact of the relocation on the employee's finances and the travail of selling and buying a home and moving the family's possessions. Even there, they may not cover all of the costs. The often generous salary increase granted to signalize the promotion (and to act as a "sweetener" to induce the employee to accept the transfer) is frequently totally eroded by the costs of relocating and settling in the new area.

More important, these programs do not address the policy issues involved in the offer and acceptance of the transfer, and they totally ignore the stress to which the employees and their families are subjected by the process. Finally, they offer nothing to sustain the employee whose transfer represents not a promotion but merely a lateral move or even a demotion that reflects a failure to adequately meet the organization's expectations.

The effects of these deficiencies are subtle, complex, and slow to become manifest. Because of a reluctance to jeopardize future promotions, they tend to be suppressed or to be attributed to causes unrelated to the transfer and the organization. Since they affect employees who are geographically dispersed and attached to different segments of the organization, they generally do not show up in the usual statistics and reviews. In any case, the employee's spouse and children who frequently bear the brunt of this problem are almost never included in the organization's records.

These effects are serious: They include suicide, broken marriages, and disturbed children. Especially when the employee is unable to register complaints against the organization, they lead to alienation, frustration, and suppressed hostility which, sooner or later, show up as illness or impaired performance or both. At the very least, the employee may decide that he or she has "had it" and quit, depriving the organization of a potentially valuable manager whose training and nurture may have entailed a substantial investment.

What, then, should a relocation program include?

First, it should arrange for the employee to have greater participation and a stronger voice in deciding whether or not the transfer should be made. Even in some organizations with formal career-planning programs, the decision to offer the transfer appears to come from "higher up" with little if any explanation of how it fits into the organization's long-range plans or understanding of what it might ultimately mean to the employee's future career. There should also be a clear, explicit policy governing the consequences of an employee's decision to refuse the transfer. In many organizations, employees feel that a record of refusing or even resisting a transfer will serve as a barrier to future advancement.

Then, except for obvious crises, there should be a long lead time before the transfer is implemented. This will allow all of the necessary arrangements to be worked out in a more leisurely, less stressful manner. If this cannot be done, consideration should be given to allowing the employee a few month's leave or a short sabbatical during which the family move can be made. Too often, transferred employees must meet the challenges of the new job while being separated from their families, bearing the physical burden of commuting back and forth over distances, and dealing with the many problems involved in resettling their families.

The employees, at least, have the support provided by the continuity of similar work and their organizational relationships, unlike their wives who are being tossed (sometimes literally) into a new environment without any. Wives, especially, are often unaccustomed to carrying the major responsibility for such important decisions as selling or buying a house. Such decisions are particularly difficult for them when everything is upset and there are perhaps very young children to be cared for, their husbands are away and preoccupied with their new jobs, and they are cutting ties to friends and helpers. Husbands whose working wives are being relocated often have similar types of problems.

Accordingly, the program should provide professional counseling and support to the employee's family in adjusting to the move and settling in the new community. This involves not only such mundane, but frequently critical, matters as finding a new doctor, dentist, or lawyer or arranging the transfer of children to acceptable new schools, but also adjustment to the social structure of the new community.

Northwestern Bell Telephone Company conducted a series of workshops led by trained consultants that probed the experiences of recently transferred employees and their families. Not surprisingly, they found that the children in these families found the moves significantly more stressful than their parents, and that too often they felt left out, manipulated, and uprooted to their disadvantage. They emphasized that, wherever possible, the children should be involved in the planning, the decision making, and the tasks of moving (Olive et al., 1976).

Based on the results of this study, Northwestern Bell has installed a program that involves a "personalized" relocation service to help families adjust to their new locations, professional counseling to help individuals and families cope more effectively with the stress of the transfer, and workshops in which some of the anxiety about moving can be dissipated by discussing it in the presence of skilled professionals, other families facing the same experience, and families that have already been through it.

A special problem that is being encountered more frequently is the transfer that involves one member of a two-career family. When it involves a parent and an older child, it is usually resolved by leaving the child behind. This may precipitate a premature leap to independence and self-sufficiency on the part of the child and an "empty-nest" syndrome in the parents, but with support and counseling, these problems can be weathered. When it involves a husband and wife, and especially when the employee's new location does not allow for continuation of the spouse's career, it may require professional counseling from a source perceived as neutral to work out a mutually acceptable compromise, or referral to a divorce lawyer.

In summary, relocation is a regular and increasing phenomenon in the organizational world that subjects the employees and their families to stresses that may be severe, debilitating, or chronically disabling. Many organizations have relocation programs that offer benefits and services that help the employee with the financial impact and the travail of the physical move of the household. These programs should be broadened to include policies and procedures that give the employees greater and more meaningful participation in the transfer decision and its implications, and "personalized" services supplemented as needed with professional counseling to help the employees and their families cope with the social and emotional stress generated by the move.

WOMEN AT WORK

More than ever before, women are taking and keeping jobs outside the home. While they continue to be concentrated in the white-collar and service jobs they have traditionally held, increasing numbers are entering blue-collar, craft, and technical and professional categories in which hitherto they had been rarities. Sparked by their own ambition, spurred by the women's liberation movement, and supported by the insistence of Equal Employment Opportunity compliance officers on building upward mobility into affirmative-action programs, more women are moving into supervisory and managerial positions. Eli Ginsburg, the Columbia University economist who chairs the National Commission for Manpower Policy, calls it a revolution in the roles of women that "will have an even greater impact than the rise of Communism and the development of nuclear energy."

Whether he was being prophetic or merely articulating male fears about changing roles remains to be seen. Nevertheless, the impact has been considerable: Many old myths have been exploded and stereotypes shattered (as new ones are being formed), while role ambiguity and role conflict in the job, in the home, and between them create new stress and anxiety in the workplace.

There are physical differences that make men taller, larger, and more powerful than women. They are exaggerated by cultural patterns that push boys into athletic play while young girls are involved in sedentary, more "ladylike" activities. But, as I emphasized in a recent report on employee health services for women workers, there are very few jobs that cannot be performed by women (Warshaw, 1978).

Sex differences in responses to stress and in patterns of emotional illness have been reported. For example, the physiologic studies of Dr. L. W. Sontag (1947) of the Fels Research Institute demonstrated that girls were more reactive to stress than boys but relaxed more easily and recovered from it more quickly. Many studies suggest that women are more susceptible to emotional difficulties, dwell more on their problems, are more introspective, and are more likely to be negative in their self-image. They are also said to be more prone to somatic complaints as manifestations of their psychological distress. These impressions are supported by data indicating that women make more visits to emotional health professionals and clinics, are more frequently labeled with a psychiatric diagnosis, and take many more tranquilizers and other mood-altering medications.

Yet, I wonder how much of this data is not merely a stereotyped reflection of male and female self-perceptions of their strengths and weaknesses and such prevailing clichés as "men are happier when doing and women when feeling," and women are "more proficient in social skills." How much of it is a kind of self-fulfilling prophecy arising out of deeply rooted attitudes toward women and expectations concerning them on the part of some health professionals and social scientists? And how much of it represents the fact that the traditional child-bearing and child-rearing role of women in our society imposes social and cultural stresses which men escape? In any case, although I have not had the opportunity to perform a carefully controlled study, my experience during more than three decades in occupational medicine suggests that the frequency and severity of outright mental and emotional illness is no greater among working women than among their male coworkers.

Nevertheless, there is growing evidence that the stress of the new life-styles of liberated women is having an impact. Coronary heart disease, once rarely seen among premenopausal women, is now becoming quite common. Lung cancer is on the rise among women, and recent statistics indicate that while males with peptic ulcer outnumbered females 20 to 1 three decades ago, there are now 5 to 10 women with ulcers for every 20 men. It has been suggested that these trends reflect women's greater use of cigarettes, alcohol, and caffeine rather than increases in stress, but, as is well known, excessive use of these substances is also symptomatic of stress.

Women do have more problems in their psychosocial adjustment to work. In part this reflects the fact that so many continue to bear the responsibilities for homemaking and the rearing of children. These burdens are time-consuming, distracting, and fatiguing, and are responsible for much of the increased absenteeism reported for women workers in virtually every set of data.

It has been reported that there is more stress in marriages in which the wife works. The effect of this on both husband and wife may carry over into their work situations. It may involve only the sharing of household duties, or the serious dilemma that arises when one career requires relocating to an area in which the other cannot flourish (see p. 140). Statistics indicate that divorce is more frequent among working couples, but they do not demonstrate whether the work is a cause or an effect. Many women take a job as an antidote to an uncomfortable home situation, and there are undoubtedly a good number who, once they find that they can earn money, realize that they no longer have to put up with a bad marriage for financial reasons.

Dual-career couples have been called a "corporate time bomb" because of the increased possibility of conflict-of-interest situations. This is not a problem when one spouse works in a blue-collar or clerical job, but it is frequently perceived as one when both work as professionals or as executives in important and potentially sensitive areas. Some companies have initiated policies forbidding the hiring or continuing the employment of an individual whose spouse works for a competitor, and some major accounting firms require members of their staff to sign an oath that no relatives, including spouses, are employed by the clients they serve. Such conflicts also create stress in the personal lives of the couples when, for example, they feel they must avoid "shop talk" and lock up any documents that deal with pending business matters. One salesman found that when his wife took an important job with a competing firm, it put a crimp in his practice of including her when entertaining customers and discussing business deals during cocktails and dinner.

The woman who joins an all-male work group may experience difficulty in becoming accepted as part of the group. The aggressiveness that she had to muster to get the job and her justified resentment that she had to be better qualified and accept lower pay to win it are sometimes translated into an abrasiveness that makes her hard to take.

Although I believe that its importance is overstated, sexual behavior can present problems. Women have complained of sexual harassment and intimidation by male bosses and coworkers and undoubtedly it does occur. Female seductiveness and male machismo expressed in dress, speech, and behavior sometimes do provoke difficulty, and the propinquity dictated by work situations (e.g., the man and woman who must take long business trips together and the policewoman who spends a whole shift in a squad car with her male partner) can create problems not only for the working pair but for spouses who are susceptible to jealousy. These problems usually signal the passage of outmoded sexual mores but they do sometimes disclose more fundamental "hang-ups" that may call for professional intervention.

In studying the complaints of her female patients who work, psychiatrist Ruth Moulton found that, although there is frequent overlap, they tended to form four distinctive patterns:

- Reentry anxiety to the point of panic or avoidance when a long home-bound woman returns to work
- Performance anxiety reflecting a woman's difficulty in asserting herself or her fear of success when she does
- The "good little girl's" difficulty in holding her own and demanding her rights when facing hostility
- Conflict between a woman's sense of personal identity and her professional identity in which marriage may be seen as a threat to her autonomy.

To assist women in overcoming such problems, a number of organizations have provided programs to train them to become more assertive and to reject the stereotyped expectation that they will be responsive, expressive, accommodating, nurturing, and passive. In 1974, for example, American Telephone and Telegraph turned to Martha McKay, who runs her own management-consulting firm and has been known as an activist in the women's movement, to design a management-development program for women. She first circulated a questionnaire among A.T.&T.'s women employees probing "What It's Like to Be a Woman in Management" which revealed that their most frequent difficulties were a lack of self-confidence, uncertainty about what they really wanted, and inability to cope with anger. This led to the development of the voluntary on-the-job program that she labeled "Womanagement." In addition to education about the company and its management procedures, the program offers career counseling, lunch-hour study groups to share job experiences and problems and to build social support, and three-day workshops featuring games and role-playing exercises intended to build confidence and practice strategy. A particular feature of the workshop is the feedback session in which the participants report and critique the results of their applications in their work activities of what they have learned.

About 50 percent of the eligible women participate in this voluntary program and most, it appears, have derived considerable benefit from it. McKay credits much of its success to the fact that it is a continuing program rather than a "one-shot" seminar that is out of context with the participant's job and whose benefits are quickly dissipated when she returns to it.

One problem created by the program is that some of the participants' bosses find it difficult to adjust to the women's new-found assertiveness. This has been obviated by arranging for them to exchange feedback with the women on a regular basis during and after the program.

That "all that glitters is not gold" is attested by the recent report of a government-financed study performed for the Law Enforcement Assistance Administration by researchers at the Program for Law and Society of the University of Illinois. Their calculations, based on the annual crime reports of the Federal Bureau of Investigation, indicate that while women's involvement in homicide, burglary, and robbery rose only slightly in the two decades ending in 1975, and even dropped in assault cases, the participation of women in forgery, embezzlement, fraud, and larceny has risen sharply, especially since 1967. The report attributes women's approach to equality with men in crime to the women's movement, noting that "a much greater proportion of women are working outside the home, which provides more women with greater opportunities to embezzle and commit fraud." The report is silent on the question of how many of these crimes can be ascribed to the self-assertiveness of these working women criminals.

We may take comfort, however, in the presentation at the recent annual meeting of the Aerospace Medical Association of the report by

Col. Leonard J. Kirschner, director of the student clinic at the Air Force Academy in Colorado Springs. He reported that the first two classes of women cadets have demonstrated the physical and emotional capabilities necessary to cope with the rigorous training program. A somewhat higher percentage of the women went on sick-call and had more visits to the clinic than their male classmates but, Col. Kirschner notes, their medical problems were mostly of a "relatively minor nature and have not seriously interfered with their training." Clearly, it would appear, women are taking command.

MID-LIFE CRISIS

In his pioneering studies of how people continue to change throughout their lifetimes, Yale psychologist Daniel J. Levinson focused on the "mid-life crisis," the transitions into middle age that are a part of human psychological and social development. Levinson found that adults have a "pervasive dread" of passing age forty. "People in their middle years," he wrote, "generally find it difficult to discuss the course and meaning of their lives. . . . Middle age has been one of the great taboo topics" (Levinson, 1977).

It is not taboo any longer. The work of Levinson and the other social scientists who have studied these phenomena has been popularized in Gail Sheehy's best-seller, *Passages* (1976), and in the hundreds of articles and discussions in all of the popular media that followed. By now, "mid-life crisis" has become almost a household word.

Although it generally strikes suddenly in the mid-forties or early fifties—hence the term "crisis"—it may occur earlier in adult life. It has two components, either of which may be more prominent: an awareness of physical aging, of the end of one's youth; and a realization of one's position in life, a discovery that one's career goals have changed in importance or will never be realized.

The mid-life crisis may be precipitated by an illness that is perceived as serious and potentially life-threatening, the sudden realization of a recently developed physical deficiency, a chance remark, or an unanticipated event on the job. Or it may be more gradual as career, biological, or family cues indicate that one is entering one's middle years. It is a time of self-awareness, a time of finally understanding who one is and what one has accomplished, and a time of re-evaluating old ambitions and long-standing desires. As Gail Sheehy put it, it is a time when we confront the fading purposes of old roles and glimpse our own mortality. Certainly, it is a time of great stress.

There are four patterns of response:

1   *Denial*—Some individuals reject the fact that they are middle-aged and set about proving that they are still youthful. Plastic surgery, hair dyes and transplants, new wardrobes modeled closely after those of their sons or daughters, and conversation laden with the vernacular of youth—these are among the strategies employed by the middle-aged to demonstrate that they are "with it." Many separate from spouses who now represent uncomfortable reminders of reality and seek new liaisons. The popular singles bars and discotheques are usually full of such individuals who often present singularly ludicrous and pathetic figures.

2   *Depression*—Willy Loman in Arthur Miller's "Death of a Salesman" is the tragic archetype of those who find themselves prematurely old, burned out, and unable either to accept or to cope with their aging. Unable to discard dreams that never materialized, often estranged from their children and friends, they are overwhelmed by their predicament and sink into apathy and depression.

3   *Acceptance*—Most people come more or less easily to accept the reality of the situation. They discard unrealistic and by now unattainable ambitions and develop more realistic appraisals of what their future will be like. If their jobs are not what they might have been, they rationalize their disappointments and seek satisfaction in hobbies or community activities and begin to plan for retirement.

4   *Planning a new life*—Increasingly, people are using the mid-life crisis more positively as a springboard for new careers and new life styles. Housewives whose children have matured into independent lives of their own now find themselves free to pursue careers abandoned when their first child was born. Individuals give up highly successful careers that they have ceased to enjoy to take up new kinds of work often in new locations. These people plan for a new future, seeking fresh answers to the old question, "What do I want to be when I finally grow up?" Many go back to school; a recent survey by the Bureau of Labor Statistics revealed that a record $1\frac{1}{4}$ million Americans over thirty-five years of age had enrolled in high school or college programs or were attending vocational schools.

Stress-management programs can be particularly helpful for those who are trying to cope with the stress that exists during the mid-life transitions. A number of organizations provide career counseling to establish new, perhaps more realistic goals and offer opportunities for the education and training that may be required to attain them.

Some organizations have created special programs for employees who have to be terminated when they are found to be redundant or their jobs are made obsolete by new processes or advances in technology. To help them to survive—and to keep them from "bad mouthing" the organization and impairing the morale of these remaining—some organizations have turned to "outplacement" consultants who provide varying mixtures of personal counseling, career guidance, and assistance in finding new jobs. Although the necessary skills may be found in the organization's personnel department, the shock and bitterness about being passed over or terminated frequently builds a wall between it and the individual. As an outsider, the outplacement consultant is in a better position to win the employees' confidence and help them rebuild their damaged self-image.

In large organizations with many departments and divisions, separated employees may be placed in another job in a different department in the same organization. This is called "cross placement"; it differs from an ordinary transfer in that the employee has been designated as expendable and must "sell" himself or herself to another unit of the organization. When this succeeds—and it does in approximately one out of every five cases in some organizations—both the employee and the organization benefit. The employee goes on to a new career in a familiar organization without loss or curtailment of pension and other benefits. By filling the new position from within, the organization saves severance pay and the expense of an employment agency or search firm and retains the loyalty of the employee.

Outplacement and mid-career counseling personnel can now be found in nearly every major city and at most universities. Their quality and cost vary widely. The fees (which are usually paid by the organization) range from $10 for a single interview to as much as $5,000 for a full program of testing and both group and individual counseling. Some focus on emotional difficulties, others provide coaching in career selection, resumé writing, and handling interviews. One even uses handwriting analysis as testing instrument on which advice is based. Great care should be exercised in selecting a consultant and making sure that the staff who will actually be working with the employees are competent.

To summarize, the mid-life transition is a time of great stress for many individuals that can lead to depression, dissatisfaction with their jobs and the organization, or aberrant social behavior in addition to all of the usual stress-related symptoms. It can not only impair the productivity of the individual, but also be disruptive to the organization. An effective stress-management program that includes career counseling can benefit not only the afflicted individual, but also the organization itself.

RETIREMENT

Most organizations are now aware that a gold watch and a handshake after lunch when an employee retires are no longer enough. Although today most employers are aware of the necessity for an adequate pension plan as an important inducement in recruiting and retaining valued employees, it is becoming increasingly evident that more is required. A company must also have an explicit policy that establishes eligibility criteria for various kinds of retirement benefits and also determines how retirement is to function as an instrument for orderly succession in personnel management. The company's retirement program should be supplemented by an effective counseling service to help the retiree cope with the inevitable stressors of the transition and to provide guidance on how to get the most out of retirement.

Some years ago, I was involved with an organization that had no pension program, no retirement policy, and no mandatory retirement at sixty-five or any age. Most of the managers and many of the rank-and-file employees were "old-timers." Without a pension, financial necessity forced many of the employees to continue working past the age when they would have preferred to retire. They clung to their jobs, often resorting to a variety of stratagems to maintain their importance and resist any encroachment on their "turf." They would, for example, delay important decisions to avoid or postpone any preventable risks, or at least to make certain that the blame would fall elsewhere if the decisions did not turn out well. I recall one executive who wrote several lengthy memos for his file whenever an issue arose, each advocating a different alternative. When the results became apparent, he would then circulate an "I told you so" note attached to a copy of the appropriate version of his earlier memo.

Even when these employees' loss of effectiveness became apparent, their superiors yielded to feelings of personal loyalty and found all sorts of excuses to delay actions that would lead to forced retirement or dismissal. Employees without personal means left only when they were forced to by serious illness or disability. The more capable and aggressive younger employees quickly resigned to join a competitor when it became apparent that their advancement was blocked by the lack of openings in higher positions.

As a result, the organization gradually lost ground to its competitors. As its condition became apparent, it became ready prey for "corporate raiders" who sought control of the valuable real estate and other capital assets it had accumulated in earlier years. Ultimately, it was absorbed into a conglomerate that dictated a ruthless—but necessary—"housecleaning" of all of the people who should have been retired years earlier. Needless to say, this was a catastrophic experience for most, far more painful than if it had come about in a more orderly and leisurely fashion.

This example—and there are many others—demonstrates that an effective retirement program is an essential element in the continuing vigor and vitality of the organization. Its importance is accentuated by the recently enacted federal and state laws regulating pension plans and providing alternatives for those ineligible for them, and those prohibiting discrimination on the basis of age and banning the mandatory retirement of employees when they reach the age of sixty-five. More than ever, it is necessary to have policies that will keep management young, flexible, and energetic. While most senior people can continue to make important contributions, a proper retirement program will encourage a fuller delegation of responsibilities and more careful planning for succession.

For the individual, retirement ranks high among stress-causing life events. Sociologist Z. S. Blau (1973) describes retirement as a form of "role-exit" stress that occurs whenever stable patterns of interaction or shared activities between two or more persons cease. Retirement, she notes, usually engenders feelings of depreciation, sadness, depression, and uncertainty similar in character, if not in intensity and duration, to those precipitated by the death of a loved person. "Role renewal" is the term given to a return of motivation, commitment, and the things that give meaning to life. The purpose of a retirement program is more than to provide an exit from the scene, it is to assist with the adaptations necessary for renewal.

For many people, retirement is a welcome event, the reward for years of work at jobs that have ceased to be—or never were—satisfying. For some it provides an opportunity to start a new career or to reactivate old ambitions that were sacrificed to the press of circumstances. For others, it means hard-earned leisure with freedom to travel, to pursue hobbies, and simply to relax and enjoy day-to-day living without the pressure of job responsibilities. These are the people who have planned their retirement, who have spent years in thinking about the changes it will bring and in adjusting to them.

There are many, however, who follow an exactly opposite course and refuse to think about it as long as possible. They tend to regard retirement as something that happens only to other people. These are the people who lack the resources to cope with the necessary changes and often fall prey to physical or emotional illness.

Most people approach retirement with apprehension, sometimes openly but more often muted or even concealed. They are apprehensive for a number of reasons:

1 *Financial concerns:* Will retirement income remain adequate, not only for subsistence, but for social activity, travel, and other pleasures? Too many have seen the purchasing power of seemingly magnificent pensions dwindle under the erosive effects of inflation.

2 *Loss of status:* Work is a central part of life for many individuals. Being ousted from it while still enterprising and vigorous can seem to them a sentence to uselessness and dependency. It means a loss of the respect of others for filling a role and doing a job adequately, an impairment of self-image that can lead to despair.

3 *Loss of social support:* For many, the companionship of fellow workers provided attention and support that was denied them in the home and not available in the community. The loneliness of those who have made no friendships outside of their work group and who cannot fall back on an immediate family circle for company can be demoralizing.

4 *Too much time:* How to fill the new-found leisure time is a difficult problem for many retirees.

5 *Concern over health:* To many, reaching retirement is a symbol of old age that makes illness more likely and more debilitating.

The preservation of health status and the availability of affordable medical services becomes a great source of worry for them.

The relative importance of these concerns varies among individuals. And there are other concerns that also must be taken into account. In the two-career family, one may be forced to retire while his or her spouse must continue to work to satisfy different criteria for retirement. Sometimes the entrepreneur or professional person has no one to take over a successful business or practice and just can't abandon it and let it wither and die. And sometimes an individual who wishes to retire must be persuaded to postpone it because the organization still needs his or her know-how and experience.

In the spring of 1975, the Institute of Labor and Industrial Relations of the University of Michigan and Wayne State University undertook a survey of the retirement programs maintained by the "Fortune 500," the nation's 500 largest corporations listed annually in the directory assembled and published by *Fortune*. Of the 172 companies responding, one-fourth sponsored a formal retirement program for their employees, half of which had been in operation for five years or longer. Another fourth of the respondents reported their intention to establish such a program in the next year (Prentis, 1975).

One-third of the programs simply provided printed information on retirement benefits, Social Security, Medicare, and company insurance plans. The remainder provided information on a wide range of topics including wills and estates, nutrition and personal health, living arrangements, and leisure interests. About one-third of the respondents offered one-to-one counseling, while a simular proportion conducted group discussions as supplements to the distribution of printed materials.

Most programs were conducted on company premises, about two-thirds during working hours. Although half the companies used an outside consultant to develop the program, nearly all were run by company personnel, in most instances by a person or department with full-time responsibility for developing and operating it.

Employee participation was almost always voluntary with eligibility commencing when the employee reached the age of sixty, about five years prior to normal retirement. Increasingly, however, with the growing popularity of early retirement, companies are allowing employees to enroll at age fifty-five or earlier.

The advantages of such programs to the employees facing retirement are obvious. Almost unanimously, the personnel directors expressed the belief that company sponsorship of the program enhanced the organization's image by demonstrating its concern for its employees' welfare. About half maintained that these programs led to increased morale and increased productivity among the workers. They also found them helpful in softening the impact of nonvoluntary retirement situations.

The Survey report offers some suggestions for establishing preretirement programs that should enhance their benefit to both employees and the organization:

1 Employees should be encouraged to participate in designing the program to be sure that it will meet their needs.

2 The program should allow enrollment at a younger age, fifty-five or earlier, so that it will be available to early retirees at least five years prior to their planned departure.

3 The program should be operated on a continuous basis by trained company personnel or outside professionals. Ideally, it should be available to all employees on a demand basis as their need for it arises.

4 The program should be open to already retired employees who missed the opportunity to enroll while still working, and those who have encountered unanticipated problems with which they would like to help.

5 The results of the program should be evaluated continuously to be sure that it is meeting the needs, interests, and goals of both the employee and the organization.

Several years ago, the Occupational Psychiatry Group, a small informal group of New York City psychiatrists active in counseling individuals and/or organizations with work-related problems and occupational physicians interested in the emotional aspects of their employee health services, devoted one of its regular meetings to preretirement programs. At one point in the discussion, when the group was asked to indicate if the organizations with which they were affiliated had ever had a preretirement program, a forest of hands went up. This was followed by the query, "How many still have these programs?" and all but two of the hands came down. The reasons for discontinuing the programs varied. Among those mentioned were lack of employee demand and interest, a need to cut costs, and departure of the staff person who had conducted the program. The major reason, however, was dissatisfaction with the program, in most instances a prepackaged mélange of pamphlets, magazines, and "canned" presentations dealing generally and impersonally with various retirement problems.

This prompts a most important addition to the suggestions developed by the *Fortune* "500" study: The program should be personalized to help each participant with the problems that concern him or her as well as providing generally useful information. One way of doing this is to provide a "smorgasbord" of information materials from which participants can select those that interest them, supplemented by access to individualized professional guidance on questions that remain unanswered. Group sessions should be held at a convenient time and place so that employees' spouses can be invited to attend. Spouses should also be allowed to join the employee in the individual counseling sessions when they are involved in the subjects being discussed. Present retirees should be encouraged to attend the group sessions not only to have their problems solved but to share their experiences, their successes and their disappointments, with those about to follow them into retirement.

Consideration might also be given to the kind of loaned personnel program that the Equitable Life Assurance Society has operated for some years with notable success. Headed by a retired personnel officer and staffed by an individual in the Corporate Services area, this program makes the services of retirees available without cost to public service agencies and organizations. The Equitable pays all the costs of the program which include very modest honoraria to the people on loan that cover any out-of-pocket and personal expenses. The program is entirely voluntary and every effort is made to match the location and kind of work required with the employee's interests, capabilities, and desires. The jobs have included clerical work, accounting, auditing, consulting in financial management for smaller voluntary agencies, tutoring disadvantaged school children with learning disabilities, and volunteer work with a number of governmental agencies. As a rule, the assignments are part-time, when possible on a schedule that makes commuting most convenient. Most of the assignments are for limited terms, but a few have expanded into long-term full-time jobs. The program has proved to be so valuable a public service that, on a number of occasions, when a needed type of expertise was not available among the retirees who had registered with the program, the Equitable has temporarily detached active employees for loaned assignments, continuing their salary and all benefits until they return to their regular jobs.

Retirement is a relatively new social phenomenon. Throughout the world, for most of its history, old age has been defined physiologically. People retired when they could no longer do a full day's work. Human life expectancy and family life were such that retired individuals were nurtured and respected. Since the beginning of the twentieth century, life span has been lengthening. We now define "old age" arbitrarily by the calendar. Skills and experience are rapidly made obsolete by advances in technology, new industries, and new patterns of organization. As a result, being old has become progressively "devalued" while work is increasingly becoming a means to an end rather than an end in itself. Instead of being cared for, retired persons now have to make their own decisions with respect to the many new options now available to them. As retirement approaches, these decisions become more urgent and important and more stressful. Since the circumstances under which they arise and the framework in which they must be made are determined by the work environment and the policies of the organization, attitudes are formed that affect both work capacity prior to retirement and relationships with the organization after it has begun.

Retirement is a stressor for organizations as well. They can no longer afford to just let it happen but must establish policies that make it an effective tool to guarantee the vigor and flexibility of its management.

In summary, therefore, retirement is a critical time of change that puts employees and organizations under great stress; the well-being of both is determined by how well they cope with it.

REFERENCES

Blau, Z. S. (1973). *Old Age in a Changing Society.* New York: New Viewpoints.

Levi, L. (1978). *Society Stress and Disease, Vol IV: Working Life.* London: Oxford University Press.

Levinson, D. J. (1977). *The Seasons of a Man's Life.* New York: Knopf.

Moulton, R. (1977). Some effects of the new feminism. *Amer. J. Psychiatry* **134**:1.

Olive, L. E.; J. E. Kelsey; N. J. Visser; and R. T. Daly (Aug. 1976). Moving as perceived by executives and their families. *J. Occup. Med.* 18:546–550.

Prentis, R. S. (1975). *National Survey of Fortune's "500" Preretirement Plans and Policies.* Ann Arbor and Detroit: Institute of Labor and Industrial Relations, University of Michigan and Wayne State University.

Sheehy, G. (1976). *Passages.* New York, E. P. Dutton.

Sontag, L. W. (1947). Physiological factors and personality in children. *Child Development* 18:185–189.

Tasto, D. L., and M. J. Colligan (1977). *Shift Work Practices in the United States.* Washington D.C.: U.S. Government Printing Office, DHEW (NIOSH) Publication No. 77-148.

Warshaw, L. J. (Oct. 1978). Employee health services for women workers. *Preventive Medicine* 7:365–393.

PART IV
COPING AND PREVENTING

11

MECHANISMS FOR COPING WITH STRESS

Scarcely an issue of a business magazine or newsletter crosses my desk that does not contain at least one article describing techniques of coping with the effects of occupational stress on individuals' well-being and productivity. They range from quiet prayer to screaming and pounding on the floor of a padded, sound-proof chamber; from conventional one-to-one counseling to the most *outre* forms of group "seminars"; from stationary bicycles to computers for charting biorhythms. One of which I'm particularly fond is the Executive Teddy Bear, a cuddly companion who says when its string is pulled: "You are a born leader!" and, "There's nothing you can't do!" and, "You are a winner, Teddy knows!"

Some are aimed at the elimination or control of sources of stress, some at neutralizing its impact, and others at making the individual more resistant or better able to cope with it. Most of these are essentially individual and private, and since they are usually operative entirely outside of the work setting, they should not concern the organization. However, since many affect the individual's work attitudes and capacity, managers should be cognizant of them.

Other techniques are aimed specifically at the individual's adaptation to work-related stressors. Some of these are suitable for implementation in the workplace, and managers are frequently besieged by individuals asking for or seeking to provide such services. Indeed, many organizations already do offer them.

Astonishingly, they all work—in some places, with some people, and at some times. Which should managers consider installing or adopting within their organizations?

Ideally, the choice will be made by the professional responsible for directing the organization's stress-management program or the consultant retained to assist employees with emotional and behavioral problems. He or she will also prescribe the mechanism for restricting its use to individuals most likely to be benefited. The alternative is to make it freely available to all employees on the assumption that those who are benefited will continue to use it while those who are not will drop out. The disadvantage to this approach is that the desired improvement is often slow to appear and individuals who might ultimately derive great benefit may become discouraged and quit.

The following brief and incomplete catalogue will attempt to describe those mechanisms for coping with stress that are suitable for implementation in the workplace.

MEDICAL THERAPY

The medical therapy of stress-related problems comprises explanation to provide understanding of how stress produces its effects, reassurance, and, much too frequently, the prescription of tranquilizers and other mood-altering medications. It is (It should be!) the major activity of an employee health facility since the great bulk of the complaints from which employees seek relief are reactions to stress. Since all of the medications customarily prescribed have a greater or lesser effect on alertness, reaction time, coordination, etc., they are of concern to the organization when taken by persons in jobs where safety hinges on their vigilance and appropriate response. They cause concern also because of the number of individuals who become habituated to their use or misuse them (see section on drug abuse, p. 150).

When this palliative form of medical therapy does not suffice, the individual is referred for counseling or more intensive psychiatric therapy. Short-term counseling can be provided by the stress-management program, but when it is not available, acceptable, or adequate, the individual is referred outside the organization to resources in the community. This, of course, may complicate matters in the work situation. The difficulties include time lost to keep appointments; the therapist's unfamiliarity with the individual's work and the role it may play in his or her difficulty; poor communication between the therapist and those in the organization concerned with the individual; the costs of treatment, especially when their coverage under the organization's insured benefits program is limited; and the rehabilitation and reentry of the individual who had to take sick leave. Unless properly managed, these can have an adverse effect on both the individual and the organization.

GROUP APPROACHES

Group approaches to the alleviation of stress are economical in that they extend their benefits to many more than can be accommodated on a one-to-one basis. They are often more effective not only because peer pressure represents a powerful motivating mechanism, but because of the social support the group provides. They take a variety of forms, many of which are quite well-suited for the work setting; perhaps the best-known and most successful of these is Alcoholics Anonymous. Some address specific problems: control of weight, smoking, high blood pressure, drug abuse, etc. Others have a more general focus: meditation, Yoga, assertiveness training, physical exercise, etc. In most instances, such group programs are provided outside of regular working hours and participating employees are often required to pay part of the cost. A frequent dilemma is the choice between limiting participation to those who clearly need the treatment or making it available on a first-come, first-served basis to everyone.

Since, when the organization provides the program it inevitably assumes responsibility for its quality and any inadvertent ill effects, careful attention must be paid to the qualifications and performance of those staffing it. Many an organization has "bought" a program from a well-accredited professional or group only to find that its delivery was delegated to a person with minimal qualifications, if any, and little experience.

EXERCISE

During the past twenty years, exercise has become an increasingly popular part of American life. It is estimated that well over one-third of the adults in this country are now participating in some kind of regular exercise activity, and many organizations are creating facilities and offering formal programs in the workplace.

Under the influence of psychogenic stressors, tension and rigidity develop in the muscles of the body, especially those of the neck, shoulders, and lower back. This leads to fatigue, stiffness, and aching, which set the stage for injury to the muscles and their ligamentous attachments. "Tension" headache is usually a reflection of pain in the muscles of the back of the neck and scalp. "Stiff neck" is a common stress syndrome. Many of the painful shoulder syndromes are created when tension and spasm of the muscles in the neck "pinch" the nerve roots as they exit from the spinal column. Most instances of backache have little or no relationship to X ray findings of congenital defects or arthritis of the spine; instead, they reflect the effects of stress on the muscles and ligaments upon which the functional integrity of the spine depend (see pp. 111ff).

Almost every form of exercise will act as an antidote to stress reactions if practiced regularly. Perhaps the only exceptions are competitive sports and games for those people who become obsessive about achieving a standard of performance or compulsive about winning. For such individuals, recreational athletic activities can become sources of stress no less potent than work or family life. For most, however, these activities provide distraction, relaxation, and a sense of well-being. In addition, there are the special benefits associated with particular forms of exercise.

The many forms of exercise activity can be classified into the following broad categories. Most balanced programs combine examples from each.

1   *Sports and recreational activities:* Many organizations mount extensive programs of sports and recreational activities. These range from bowling leagues to what amounts to semiprofessional teams composed of employees hired more for their athletic prowess than for any other capabilities they might have. Most often, the participants in these programs are people who would probably be exercising anyway. The activities are much more convenient and less expensive when provided by the organization on or near the premises and they do have considerable social value. They also can relieve stress. I recall one individual who found his bowling league a splendid outlet for all of the pent-up hostility he'd accumulated during the week. He simply projected the face of his boss or some other person who had been irritating him on to the head pin and let fly, putting all the force he could muster into his delivery. Even though his score wasn't very high, the crash of the pins was a great source of satisfaction.

2   *Aerobic or cardiovascular fitness:*   Although final proof is not yet at hand, there is compelling evidence that regular periods of high energy output will protect against coronary mortality directly as well as through reducing the influence of such high-risk factors of coronary heart disease as hypertension and elevated blood lipids. Many epidemiologic studies have shown that people who are regularly active tend to live longer than those who are physically inactive.

Aerobic exercise is any rhythmic activity that promotes a sustained increase in heart rate, respiration, and muscle metabolism. The body adapts to the added demands of such exercise by improved heart and lung function and increased muscular endurance.

Most authorities agree that it is advisable for all individuals over thirty-five years of age to have a complete medical evaluation, including an exercise-stress test (electrocardiograms and other measurements made before, during, and following a period of calibrated exercise) before entering an exercise program. On the basis of the results, an exercise prescription can be developed that specifies the intensity of exercise (the heart-rate increase) to be attained, its duration (how long the elevated heart rate should be maintained), and its frequency (how many exercise sessions a week). The entire period may be spent at one exercise, such as jogging, cycling, or swimming, or at a sequence of varied activities.

The National Aeronautics and Space Administration headquarters in Washington, D.C., inaugurated such a program in 1968 and many organizations have followed suit. In the New York City area alone, for example, Mobil Oil, the Chase Manhattan Bank, Exxon, New York Life, the New York Telephone Company, and General Foods are among those that have installed facilities specially equipped for aerobic exercise training. Equitable Life, Time, Inc., McGraw-Hill, and others offer employees such programs at a nearby commercial facility that provides a professionally supervised aerobic exercise program. Xerox Corporation has developed for its own employees and for marketing to other organizations a do-it-yourself approach which it calls the Xerox Health Management Program. This includes a manual for periodic self-screening and self-testing, a "Fitbook" with illustrated exercise instructions, and forms for recording activities and their results.* Participants in these programs who achieve and maintain their target levels of cardiovascular fitness have reported en-

---

* Xerox Health Management Program, Xerox Corporation, Stamford, Conn 06904.

hanced work capacity and productivity, reduced absenteeism, and improved physical and mental well-being.

3 *Muscular fitness and strength:* Programs to develop and maintain muscular strength and endurance generally involve exercises of specific muscles or groups of muscles against increasing resistance by using weights, pulleys, or a special apparatus. While these exercises are useful for "body-building," they offer little benefit toward cardiovascular fitness. In fact, if performed improperly, they may cause potentially serious reactions in certain individuals.

4 *Tension-relieving exercises:* Almost every form of mild exercise performed regularly and rhythmically is useful in relieving the tension produced by stress. Calisthenics performed during several daily "exercise breaks" are a regular routine in some work organizations. From China has come Tai Chi Chuang, a sequence of slow, graceful and fluid movements in which concentration on the movement produces mental as well as physical relaxation. Yoga combines mysticism and meditation with exercises that produce relaxation as well as increasing flexibility and muscle strength. Some organizations have found dance classes to be quite popular with female employees.

Lilias Folan, nationally known through her popular television series, "Lilias, Yoga and You," seen daily on PBS stations throughout the country, has developed a five-minute series of tension-relieving exercises that can be done discreetly while at one's desk, on the phone, or even in a board meeting. These exercises have been incorporated into a twelve-page illustrated booklet distributed by the Westinghouse Architectural Systems Division.*

There are many problems in providing an in-house exercise program for employees beyond the costs of the space and equipment. Will it be open to both men and women? To employees on all levels or only to executives? Will it be supervised by those responsible for recreational activities or by the staff of the employee health service? Will employees be allowed to exercise on their own or will there be specified entrance requirements and supervision during exercise sessions? Will the program cater to those with developed athletic ability, or will it focus on those who require encouragement and special coaching?

---

* Folan, L., *Sitting Pretty*. Distributed by Westinghouse Architectural Systems Division, 4300 36th Street, S.E., Grand Rapids, Michigan 49508.

One caveat which even well-trained physical instructors frequently overlook is the need for sedentary individuals, especially those who are older, to condition themselves for full participation in the program. Failure to heed this can produce musculoskeletal or other difficulties that not only may be temporarily disabling, but often lead to quitting the program. Special attention should also be paid to warm-up and cool-down routines before and after performing the exercises, and to the inclusion of relaxation training and exercises that promote flexibility and joint movements as well as those that strengthen muscles and expend energy.

While some organizations have installed impressively elaborate exercise facilities on their premises, many provide excellent programs using a classroom or some other open area, a rooftop, or a parking lot. It is important to recognize that the benefits of the program depend less on the amount and sophistication of the equipment than on the knowledge and leadership skills of the staff persons running it.

DIET

Special diets, often supported with evangelical zeal by their proponents, have been advocated for the relief of stress reactions. Some are based on the theory that susceptibility to stressors is caused by allergy to certain elements in the diet or the toxic effects of the small amount of additives, insecticides, and other pollutants present in foodstuffs. Others are based on the theory that stress puts additional demands on the body that are not met by the "normal" diet and that require the "antistress factors" found in certain foods and supplements of extra vitamins. The "Megavitamin" regimen, which calls for massive doses of vitamins, especially Vitamin C, is an example of the latter. All these "stress" diets are controversial, and it would seem prudent for the organization, to say nothing of individuals, not to become committed to any of them.

The organization should, however, be interested in what its employees eat and take pains to provide a balanced selection of foods in its in-plant food-service facility. A frequent valid complaint is the failure to stock anything but "junk foods" in the vending machines that provide snacks and coffee breaks. In organizations where employees bring their own lunches to eat at the work site, proper attention should be paid to the wash-up routine and other steps to prevent contamination of the workers' food by the toxic chemicals and other substances with which they may have been working.

MEDITATION AND RELAXATION

The benefits of muscular relaxation and mental concentration in relieving anxiety and tension, facilitating coordination and performance, and producing a general feeling of well-being have been known for centuries. In one form or another, techniques to accomplish this are found in every culture. They range from the rituals of repeated prayers and incantations found in primitive and ancient religions to the distinctive patterns of contortions exhibited by professional baseball players just before they step into the batter's box and the "psyching up" routines practiced by weight lifters before beginning an effort.

Very early in my occupational health practice, I encountered employees who, with or without external stimuli, gradually built up tension and anxiety to and beyond the point of interfering with their performance and producing discomfort. Recognizing the utter uselessness of reassurances that they were physically sound and the sheer futility of the injunction to "just relax," which most of them had heard many times, I devised a little ritual that proved most beneficial. I would have them stand up if they customarily sat, or sit down if they generally stood or walked about while working. Then, with eyes closed, they practiced breathing in and out to a slow rhythmic cadence, precisely in time to a silent or audible count until they reached one hundred or some other "major number"—in difficult cases, I had them start high and count back until they reached zero. Often, the breathing exercise was accompanied by arm, shoulder, and neck movements that slowly and gently alternated flexion and extension.

The whole procedure required from five to ten minutes and was repeated several times a day on a regularly scheduled basis and at any other time that it seemed to be indicated. During the exercise period, no calls were taken or interruptions allowed. To make sure that the prescribed schedule was kept, the individual was asked to set an alarm clock or to give one to his or her secretary or a coworker who could be persuaded to monitor this performance.

I have no recollection of where I learned about this remedy; since then, I have encountered more than a few clinicians who prescribe it in one form or another. It seemed like such a simple, commonsense procedure that I never did any research to find out how often and why it worked. The important thing is that whenever it was practiced faithfully, the results were almost uniformly good. Recently, more than two decades after I taught it to them, I met two people who reported that they still benefit from its use.

In 1959, Maharishi Mahesh Yogi introduced his program of Transcendental Meditation (TM) to the Western world, and by the early 1970s an estimated 10,000 persons were joining the program each month in the United States alone. Schools and training programs carried the program to every part of the country and stories about it were featured by all of the media. It even became fodder for comedians as exemplified by a cartoon showing a "visiting fireman" entering a work room where employees were sprawled about in all kinds of limp, relaxed positions while his guide says in the caption, "They're not asleep, they're just meditating!"

TM is purveyed with an aura of mysticism and mystery. Each subject must pay a fee to learn the technique in private from an approved TM instructor and must sign a contract promising not to reveal the secrets of the training ritual.

Because of the mysticism derived from Hindu religions and certain features of its ritual, many people find TM objectionable. Some have even attacked it for being idolatrous and have made protests against proposals to introduce it into public schools. In its defense, its proponents produce statements from Catholic and other members of the clergy claiming that TM enhances people's relationship with God and the practice of their faith.

TM involves two daily twenty-minute periods of meditation. It requires a quiet environment with no distracting stimuli, the assumption of a comfortable position that involves little or no muscular work, the repetition of the *mantra*, a sound or a word selected by the instructor and presented as an exclusive gift, and the development of a passive attitude.

The subjective feelings produced by this ritual vary considerably. Some experience simply a feeling of restfulness and quiet, some describe a sense of well-being and pleasure, and others report a feeling of deep relaxation that borders on ecstasy.

The physiologic effects also vary considerably both in form and degree. The most significant finding is a decrease of about 10 to 20 percent in oxygen consumption (this is seen in sleep, but the drop is neither as great nor as rapid) indicating a lowering of body metabolism. The rate and depth of respiration decline and cardiac output drops as a result of a slower heart rate and reduced volume with each beat. Blood pressure drops—more markedly if it is high—and there is evidence of redistribution of the blood in the circulation. Electrical resistance of the skin rises—it is known to fall with anxiety—and there are changes in brain-wave patterns that are quite different from those recorded during sleep or hypnosis.

The chief benefit claimed for TM is that it eases stress. It has been claimed to be helpful in improving job performance and productivity, normalizing high blood pressure, healing peptic ulcers, curing insomnia and drug addiction, and relieving a host of psychophysiologic disorders.

Dr. Herbert Benson and his associates at the Harvard Medical School and Boston's Beth Israel Hospital have studied TM shorn of its Hindu mysticism and ritual. Calling it the "Relaxation Response," they have confirmed the physiological effects and its value in reducing tension. They advocate incorporating it into one's life-style, claiming that after two or three weeks, the individual will be more at ease, will be better able to cope with work problems, and will be a better person! Benson has initiated relaxation-response programs in a number of business organizations and reports that some are so pleased with the results that they are considering replacing their coffee breaks with "relaxation-response breaks." With the publication of his *The Relaxation Response* (1975) and its subsequent appearance in paperback, supplemented by countless articles and interviews describing its content, the popularity of the relaxation response has soared. It appears to work no differently from and to be no less effective than TM, and it can be learned without any mystery and without paying any fee or signing a contract.

A variation on this theme has been advanced by Patricia Carrington, Ph.D., a Princeton psychologist who has made an extensive study of meditation and whose recently published book, *Freedom in Meditation* (1977), contains probably the most lucid discussion of its mechanism, effects, and techniques. Her system, called "Clinically Standardized Meditation," falls somewhere between TM and Benson's relaxation response. The technique is fundamentally common to all three. Like Benson, Dr. Carrington brushes aside the mysticism, the Hindu ritual, and the secretiveness of TM. Like TM, however, she believes that meditation can be learned more quickly and effectively if taught by an experienced and qualified person—someone she calls the "supervisor."

To assist people in mastering her approach to meditation, she has published a "Self-Regulating Course" consisting of a set of instructional audiotapes and a semiprogrammed instruction text known as the "Course Workbook." These are supplemented by an instructor's manual containing advice on teaching people how to use the course and on stimulating their motivation to continue meditating on a regular basis.

Essentially, she believes, most people can learn the technique of mediation in a few minutes. But she finds that without systematic training in its proper use, and without creating and sustaining the motivation to keep at it until it becomes a part of daily life, there will be a high rate of attrition and most people will stop practicing it.

Dr. Carrington warns that individuals taking medication for endocrine or metabolic disorders, for the control of pain, or for psychiatric disorders should be carefully observed by a physician familiar with the effects of meditation. Persons balanced on regular doses of insulin, thyroid preparations, or antihypertensive drugs may require a reduction in their doses while engaging in the regular practice of meditation. Failure to make such adjustments may lead to toxicity from a dose that previously was well tolerated.

In addition, she cautions, individuals with physical or emotional difficulties requiring therapeutic intervention should be under the care of a competent health professional, preferably one who is familiar with the technique of meditation. Meditation can be used in conjunction with other forms of therapy, but, she emphasizes, it cannot replace competent medical care.

A number of authors have called attention to the danger of excessive practice of meditation. When used for many hours a day over a period of several days, individuals have been observed to withdraw from the everyday world and develop symptoms ranging from insomnia to outright hallucinations. In describing this syndrome, however, Dr. Benson emphasizes that it is difficult to determine how much it is a reflection of the excessive use of meditation and how much is attributable to the susceptibility of the individual. Many people with preexisting psychiatric problems, he notes, are drawn to any technique that evangelistically promises relief from stress and tension. However, he feels, it is unlikely that the exercise of meditation for twenty to thirty minutes once or twice a day would do any more harm than spending an equivalent time at prayer (Benson, 1974).

Over the years, the search for better ways to combat stress has spawned an ever-growing number of techniques for meditation and relaxation. Anthrocentric Medication, Autogenic Training, Progressive Relaxation, Self-Directed Relaxation, the controlled breathing of Hatha Yoga, Gestalt Body Awareness—these are but a few that have won practitioners, promoters, and participants. They all work—in some people, some of the time. The common denominator is that individuals can learn to influence their body functions to relieve the effects of stress and anxiety. The techniques vary in complexity, but they are not difficult to master. Some require an instructor, trainer, or therapist, but to derive full benefit they must be practiced by the individual regularly as a part of daily life. Much more research is needed to determine how much of the benefit is attributable to the physiologic changes, how much to the concurrent abandonment of bad habits and unhealthy practices, and how much to the placebo effect (see p. 45).

Although such programs have been embraced by some organizations, their role in the work setting remains to be clarified. They are relatively inocuous, and quite inexpensive (the largest cost is employee time). However, they do not address the *causes* of stress and cannot serve as a total replacement for skilled professional intervention in treating its effects.

BIOFEEDBACK

Biofeedback is simply instrumentation that gives people information about what is going on in their bodies. A bathroom scale, a clinical thermometer, a meter that counts the pulse rate—these are examples of biofeedback. An even more classic example is the polygraph, or "lie detector," which uses changes in body functions to identify words or questions that are particularly stressful for the subject.

It had long been thought that most basic body functions such as breathing, heart rate, blood pressure, skin temperature, release of certain hormones, bowel activity, and muscle tension were entirely involuntary, being regulated autonomously by the lower, more primitive centers in the brain and nervous system. Recent research has demonstrated anatomic and functional connections between these centers and the cerebral cortex, the brain's highest level, and has shown that the brain can learn to control these functions at will. These functions are involved in the body's responses to stressors and, when

extreme or sustained, can develop a momentum of their own or establish a vicious cycle which ultimately leads to the stress-related difficulties described earlier. By learning to control them, the pathway is
blocked and the ill effects are prevented. This does nothing to reduce
or modify the stress, but it does rob it of its adverse effects. Biofeedback training is the program through which the individual learns to
exercise that control.

Some proponents of biofeedback training claim that it does more.
Body and mind are so closely intertwined, they say, that the self-
regulation of physiological functions leads to an increase in self-
awareness which in turn enables people to solve their problems. This
may be so, but, at least in most instances of more serious difficulty,
some form of psychotherapy is required to produce the changes in perception that enable individuals to view their stressful relationships in a
more benign light.

A complete biofeedback laboratory contains a battery of measuring capabilities: skin temperature, sweating, muscle tension, heart
rate, blood pressure, brain waves, intestinal movements, etc. They
may measure the function directly, as with a pulse meter, or indirectly
by a physiologically associated reaction, such as the changes in
resistance of the skin that reflect the activity of the sympathetic nervous system which also regulates blood pressure. The trainer generally tries to teach the subject to recognize the feelings that regularly ac-
company desired or undesired levels of function so that the subject can
be aware of their intensity when away from the equipment. Once this
is learned, the subject no longer needs the equipment except for an occasional test to verify the validity of his or her observations. In essence, biofeedback training is analogous to the golf pro who uses
mirrors and a TV tape recorder to help individuals to smooth out their
swing by learning better muscle control and coordination. Once they
have it, they need only practice it regularly enough to continue to
enjoy its beneficial effect on their golf game.

Biofeedback needs much more research to develop its full range
of usefulness and to delineate its limitations. In fact, HEW's recent up-
date of the manual it issues to Medicare carriers lists biofeedback
therapy in the category of nonreimbursable treatments on the ground
that it is still experimental. In their review of its applications, Drs.
Miller and Dworkin (1977) of the Rockefeller University, pointing out
the possibility of the placebo effect (see p. 45) call for more elaborate
controls and more careful evaluation of its use. They emphasize that

the apparently satisfactory effect may be illusory, citing the observation that Yoga exercises which appear to stop the heart for brief periods do make the pulse and heart sounds disappear, but if an electrocardiogram is taken during the maneuver the heart is found to be beating very rapidly. They also point out that individuals can learn to control certain physiologic functions by maneuvers that evoke certain reflexes. For example, an individual subject to attacks of rapid heart action can learn to abort them by taking a sudden deep breath in a way that stimulates certain nerve reflexes which slow the heart. This is an important and valuable learned effect, but it is not voluntary control of the automatic nervous system. Finally, emphasizing the complexity of the problem, others have noted that when one pathway for responses to stress is blocked by voluntary or other forms of control, stress symptoms may appear in a different, apparently unrelated body function.

Yet, Miller and Dworkin agree, certain applications of biofeedback training have yielded such good results that further evaluation of its utility is to be encouraged.

Dr. James Manuso, the clinical psychologist who directs the emotional health program at the Home Office of the Equitable Life Assurance Society, installed a biofeedback laboratory over a year ago. To my knowledge, this was the first to be created in the work setting. The initial results have been most promising; several individuals have been helped to overcome difficulties that resisted other forms of intervention. It is also quite popular—there is now a waiting list to use it. Although Dr. Manuso is quite pleased with what he has accomplished with it, he is still waiting to accumulate a sufficiently large experience and a long enough follow-up before reaching any definitive conclusions about its value.

RECREATIONAL ACTIVITIES

Although not usually pictured as such, the after-hours recreational programs conducted by many organizations are useful aids in coping with work-related stress. In addition to providing diversion, entertainment, and the satisfaction of accomplishment, they provide for personal interaction among people with similar interests, which often provides the social support needed to cope with many forms of stress. There is always the danger of allowing the formation of cliques and cults that can be a source of stress for those not involved, but this is easily handled by controlling the criteria for participation and the calibre of the leadership.

CAREER COUNSELING

A rather common stress pattern is exhibited by employees who find themselves in jobs for which they are not really suited or in which they see no future. Often they are good performers and are considered valuable employees. As a rule, their problem is not resolved by modifying the disagreeable job to make it more palatable—they are the proverbial "square pegs." Essentially, they face three options: to suffer the stress of increasing dissatisfaction which leads ultimately to performance that is below par and the other adverse effects of maladaption to stress; to endure the job, performing just well enough to get by while seeking sources of personal satisfaction and self-esteem outside the work situation; or to quit and try a different kind of work elsewhere. A program of career counseling that will help such individuals assess their interests and capabilities and guide them to new opportunities to apply them can be of enormous benefit. In many instances, they can be introduced to other parts of the organization and arrangements can be made for any training that they may require to make the transition. The counselor must be free to recommend, when necessary, that the individual would be better off in another organization.

BIORHYTHMS

According to biorhythms, a fad that is enjoying increasing popularity as this is written, every individual has three cycles—physical, emotional, and intellectual—that govern his or her capabilities and well-being. Each begins at birth and runs unvaryingly throughout life: the physical for twenty-three days, the emotional for twenty-eight days, and the intellectual for thirty-three days. Each starts with a "positive" phase that peaks at about one-fourth of the cycle. The curve then declines, crossing the baseline at the midpoint to enter the "negative" phase. This peaks at the three-quarter point and the curve gradually rises to cross the baseline at the end of the period. Then, the cycle repeats itself. Since the cycles have different timetables, they are in varying phases on any given day.

We are at our best when the appropriate cycle is at its peak. At the physical high, we are full of energy and stamina, strong and well-coordinated. At its low, we are weak, fatigue easily, and have little resistance to disease. The emotional high is characterized by cheerfulness, creativity, awareness, and self-confidence. When that curve ebbs, we tend to be moody, irritable, and depressed. The intellectual peak is accompanied by improved memory and reasoning power, alertness, and ambition. At the intellectual ebb, concentration and memory are poor and we are easily distracted and more likely to use poor judgment.

The "critical days" or "focus" phases are those on which the curve crosses the baseline—in either direction. Then, our powers are in flux or transition and things are most liable to go wrong. Everything is unstable and one is more likely to get sick, make errors, or have an accident.

According to the biorhythm theory, individuals are vulnerable when any of their curves are crossing the baseline, but the most critical time of all is when all three of the curves are at the baseline on the same day. That is the time for extra care if serious accidents or other misfortunes are to be prevented.

Biorhythms had their origin at the close of the nineteenth century when two doctors, apparently working independently in Vienna and Berlin, described the physical and emotional cycles. The intellectual cycle was added in the 1920s by an Austrian engineer. Today, this has become a sizable industry. Books and pamphlets describing the theory and offering instructions for charting one's curves are available everywhere. There are services that will send subscribers personalized biorhythm calendars so that they can plan their activities on the basis of the curves' forecasts. Pocket biorhythm calculators are selling briskly and coin-activated biorhythm machines can be found in supermarkets, bars, and other public places.

Since the cycles are identical for everyone, it is easy to plot charts for other people if you know their birthdates. This system has been used by professional gamblers in calculating the odds they offer for sporting events. Using a computer program, they feed in the birthdates of key players on an athletic team and, based on information about their cycles and how they performed on particular dates in the past, forecast how the team will to do in an upcoming contest. To assist the betting fraternity, one company has produced a "Baseball Prediction Kit" containing the birthdates of prominent players along with formulas for charting their biorhythms. Sales have been so encouraging that the company is planning to market similar kits for football and other team sports.

A few doctors are using patients' biorhythms to determine when elective operations should be scheduled, and in one clinic, it is said, surgeons are asked to take holidays on their own critical days. Some marriage counselors are using couples' biorhythm charts to explain why they have frequent spats and advise them to be particularly nice to each other when the charts forecast ebb or critical days.

Industry, too, has succumbed to the biorhythm "virus," thanks to reports of air crashes and train wrecks that occurred on the critical days of the involved pilots and engineers. Several trucking firms that provided their vehicle operators with biorhythm charts and warned them to take extra care on their critical days have reported reductions in their accident rates. A.T.&T. has a program for its shared-use computer system that will provide biorhythm charts to employees who wish them. This has been used in several of its units, and the safety director of a chemical plant in Texas has used a similar computer program to forecast the critical days of its 900 employees.

The results have been far from convincing, either in forecasting the winners of athletic contests or reducing accidents in industry. A number of enthusiastic claims have been publicized, especially in advertisements for biorhythm gadgets or services, but they have proven to be either incapable of validation or gross exaggerations. Proponents of biorhythms concede that the curves are not perfect, that it is possible for individuals to be ill, depressed, or to make mistakes when they are at their peaks. Skeptics, of which there are many, label them sheer nonsense or, at best, self-fulfilling prophecies.

A number of managers, while far from sold on the biorhythm curves, have allowed their introduction on the theory that concern over critical days by the members of a work group would enhance the general level of safety consciousness and, thereby, reduce the frequency of accidents. This would be capitalizing on the "Hawthorne" effect or the placebo reaction. However, it can be argued, it could work just the opposite way: Complacency and carelessness, fostered by the conviction that nothing can go wrong on peak days, might produce just the reverse effect.

In my view, biorhythms are in the class of horoscopes and numerology. I have discussed them at such length not only to decry their popularity, but to demonstrate the necessity for managers to be critical of fads as they arise and to be sure that they are scientifically validated before considering their introduction into their organizations.

REFERENCES

Benson, H. (Aug. 1974). Your innate asset for combating stress. *Harvard Business Review* **52**:49–60.

––––––. (1975). *The Relaxation Response.* New York: Morrow.

Carrington, P. (1977). *Freedom in Meditation.* New York: Anchor/ Doubleday.

Miller, N. E. and B. R. Dworkin (June 1977). Effects of learning on visceral functions—biofeedback. *N. Engl. J. Med.* **296**:1274–1278.

12

MECHANISMS FOR PREVENTING STRESS REACTIONS

The organization would of course be better off if it could *prevent* stress reactions among its employees, and there is a growing inventory of mechanisms, programs, and activities that are supposed to do just that. Many are rediscovered models of the traditional "wheel," sometimes with a catchy new name or, even better, an acronym. Some enjoy such a wave of popularity with articles in many of the business periodicals and circuit-riding seminars that those managers who are forced to admit that their organizations have not yet adopted "whatever-it-is" are indicating that they are old-fashioned and out-of-date.

As a rule, these mechanisms are supported by testimonials, usually based on the reports of the initial effects. Rarely are there careful evaluations over time, and even more rarely are these evaluations based on suitably controlled observations. I often wonder whether the ultimate benefits justify the effort and disruption required to put them in place. One is always reminded of the "Hawthorne effect," the now-classic observation that in testing modifications of the workplace that would increase productivity, it mattered little what was done as long as it was a change and the workers involved knew that they were being measured.

This suggests one important caveat in instituting stress-reduction mechanisms, especially when they are summarily imposed by management. Workers will perceive them as a management smokescreen to obscure valid complaints that are still being ignored, or as a ploy to get more work out of them, a kind of "speed-up" without any meaningful reward. In such instances, the resulting resentment and dissatisfaction usually drive the stress level to a new high.

The solution is to move more slowly, perhaps to test the new program in a small unit or part of the organization and, not only advertise its purposes and how it will work, but allow employees to participate in tailoring the pilot experiment and evaluating its results. If the employees can be given a sense of ownership of the project, it will invariably be more effective.

The following represent a selection of some of the mechanisms that have been more successful or are currently popular.

ATTITUDE SURVEYS

Attitude surveys are used to measure employee morale and to identify aspects of the organization and conditions in the workplace that may be sources of dissatisfaction and stress. They use questionnaires or structured interviews, often conducted by persons from outside the organization to enhance confidence in the anonymity of the responses. The results can be singularly helpful in identifying existing problems and potential sore spots as well as testing the acceptability of proposed alternative solutions.

One caution: It requires sophistication and experience to design the survey, to verify the validity of the sampling techniques when the entire work force is not involved, and to analyze the significance of the results. It is often desirable to pretest the survey instrument on a small group of representative individuals to be sure that the questions are clear and unambiguous.

It should be noted that although surveys provide a mechanism for upward communication within the organization, they are temporary and often very superficial. They are much more valuable when used as a supplement to well-established channels of communication and, when repeated, as a measure of changes in attitudes over time. Also, management should keep in mind that the survey will lack credibility if the results are not made generally known within the organization or if nothing is done about items clearly identified as sources of dissatisfaction.

RAP SESSIONS

Rap sessions are meetings of one or more managers with groups of employees to discuss items of mutual interest. The group may comprise an entire work unit or representatives of particular categories of employees who share a common problem: e.g., minorities, women, or secretaries. In the latter instance, it is advisable to rotate the membership so that all the employees in that category may eventually participate.

Within reasonable constraints that are specified in prearranged ground rules, employees are usually encouraged to be open and frank without fear of reprisal. The participating managers must remain unruffled and be accurate and candid in explaining the organization's policies and positions. All questions should be answered, if not during the session then at a subsequent one or via personal communications to the persons who asked them.

When conducted without condescension and evasion, rap sessions are effective mechanisms for communicating employees' concerns and feelings to management and for managers to inform employees about the organization's goals, problems, and constraints. They provide excellent opportunities to ventilate strong feelings that create stress, whether or not they are valid. They become quite useless, however, if reprisals are taken against employees who raise sensitive subjects or express their feelings too vigorously, and if the promises made by the manager are not kept.

THE LECTURE CIRCUIT

It has become fashionable to include a lecture dealing with some aspect of stress on the programs of company meetings, especially sales meetings and industry conventions. The lecturer, often the author of a recent best-seller, presents a rapid-fire series of anecdotes and observations in which the listeners can readily identify themselves or people they know. Each item is followed by a piece of "how-to" advice that is appealing because it sounds easy to do, agrees with commonsense versions of psychodynamic theory, and, at least according to the speaker, almost always works. The talk is usually well-larded with humor and often seasoned with strong overtones of evangelism.

In a recent *New York Times* column about one of the currently popular author-lecturers, Herbert Mitgang described him as "one of the vendors of the quick fix for our psyches, (he) is a medicine man selling elixirs and himself in a tradition that goes back to the traveling carny shows of a century ago. The cure-all for the aches and pains in our heads is not a spoonful before bedtime, but a chapter of advice that oozes with self-confidence, get-up-and-go, life can be beautiful, and if not, make it so" (Mitgang, 1978).

Are these lectures worth the fees they command—as high as $10,000 for the more popular speakers? When considered on the basis of their entertainment value and the drawing power of their names in the advance programs, they probably are. When examined from the standpoint of any real effect on the well-being of the listeners, the results are mixed. Some listeners will be persuaded to order for subsequent study the books or recordings that the speaker plugs in the course of the presentation. A few may be made more aware of current difficulties and, encouraged by the up-beat tone of the talk, stimulated to consult a mental-health professional for the treatment they need. Perhaps more often, a listener may be stimulated to persuade a spouse or a coworker with manifest problems to accept recommendations to enter therapy that he or she had been resisting.

There are also adverse effects. Individuals with deep-seated problems for which skilled professional help is required may be persuaded by a fast-talking advocate of the do-it-yourself school to delay the start of therapy, or even to interrupt it. Even more damaging is that such lecturers occasionally reinforce the prejudice against individuals with emotional illnesses sometimes displayed by unsophisticated bosses and coworkers who view such problems as a sign of weakness that can be overcome by the exercise of "willpower." The facile approach to emotional well-being purveyed by these lecturers appears to confirm such attitudes, eroding further any likelihood of the person in such difficulty receiving the support and understanding that could be so helpful.

Most of the audience, however, remains untouched by these presentations. The advice is usually so superficial that it gets lost in the tide of the other presentations and convention activities. Ultimately, in some instances, their only value is that they serve as a demonstration of management's concern about the effects of stress and its readiness to do the "right thing" about it.

MANAGEMENT DEVELOPMENT

Management development is a formal program to upgrade the skills and capacities of managers and to enhance their ability to handle broader, more complex assignments. It involves long-range career planning, rotating assignments to provide varied types of experience as well as more intimate knowledge of different segments of the organization, educational activities within and outside the organization, and periodic review and appraisal. It offers the manager a pathway to promotion and continuing advancement while providing the organization with more effective managers and a line of succession. When well-rounded, the management-development program trains participants to cope with the stressors inherent in the program: rapid change, frequent relocation, the burdens on spouse and children, the competitiveness of fellow participants, and the crushing disappointment for those who fail to reach their personal goals. The manager will fail and the organization will suffer if the program does not also train the participant in the management of "people" problems and the control of stress within the organization.

ORGANIZATION DEVELOPMENT

Organization development is defined as a planned organization-wide program, managed from the top, to increase organizational effectiveness and health by a variety of interventions based on knowledge from the behavioral sciences. It is aimed at groups, not individuals, and involves all of the processes in which they are engaged and the ways in which they are related. Thus it deals with methods for planning and setting goals, decision-making processes, communication channels and styles, competition among groups, and the management of conflict. It addresses such characteristics of organizational function as the number of hierarchical levels, the span of control, and role relationships. In addition to such operational goals as improved productivity, it aims at a healthier, more flexible organization, better equipped to deal with its rapidly changing external environment and maintain an internal environment that will be less stressful and more satisfying to all its personnel.

Unfortunately, organizational development, or "O.D.," has become a "buzz-word." It is being marketed in books, lectures, and seminars as *the* answer to any and all organizational problems and often is used as a "quick fix" by those charged to solve them. It may be a significant coincidence that the same letters stand for "over-dose," the condition of drug abusers who take too much of the drug they use to feel good.

O.D. is a process that involves a long-term (at least three or more years), action-oriented commitment to change. While it deals with groups, it requires changes in the attitudes, behavior, and performance of individuals in the organization. It is self-correcting, involving constant reevaluation of the present situation, testing of alternatives, and implementation of the strategy deemed most effective.

JOB RESTRUCTURING

Job restructuring or job redesign is a substantial body of programs and activities that includes:

1 *Socio-technical Design*—Redesign of the physical and technical features of the workplace. (This is to be distinguished from ergonomics, also known as human factors, which focuses on the person-machine interface and the way work is done with the aim of easing the physical stress of work tasks and reducing the incidence of injury.)

2 *Job Enlargement*—Increasing the number and variety of tasks assigned to a particular job without requiring the exercise of any greater skill or responsibility.

3 *Job Rotation*—To relieve the monotony of doing the same thing all the time, job assignments are changed either on an ad-lib basis or in accord with a prearranged schedule. This requires no changes in design of the various jobs.

4 *Job Enrichment*—Providing more autonomy and responsibility, giving the workers a larger share in ownership of the products of their efforts. It gives employees greater control over the "flow" of their work: letting them set their own pace, establish quotas, assign schedule dates, etc. To be effective, it requires frequent feedback on their job performance.

5 *Autonomous Work Groups*—Structuring work around self-regulating work groups. Instead of a series of tasks performed sequentially by different workers, the whole sequence is assigned to the group

which, within limits set by higher management, sets its own pace and standards. Workers are free to rotate jobs within the unit, to try new tools and processes, and, again within limits, to make their own safety rules. To provide faster and more detailed information about the quantity of their work, a quality-control person is assigned to examine their output more quickly and required to report back to them.

Sometimes, when the groups are too large for effective inter-action, they are broken up into smaller teams, each performing the same sequence of tasks. In many instances, the pay-reward system is changed from an individual to a group bonus scheme. Two well-pub-licized examples of autonomous work groups are those in the Volvo automobile factory in Sweden and at the Harman International Indus-tries plant at Bolivar, Tennessee.

As might be expected, each of these approaches to job restructur-ing has its enthusiastic proponents who cite statistics demonstrating that their introduction has improved productivity, reduced accidents and machine breakdowns, improved job satisfaction, reduced absen-teeism and turnover, cut customer complaints about product quality, and reduced waste of materials. Much less is said about the fail-ures—and there have been some.

Unions often take a skeptical view of these efforts at "humanization of work." They view them as power plays by manage-ment to undermine the union's traditional posture as guardian of the workers' welfare, and point out that most of the organizations that have instituted such changes are not unionized. They regard increased job satisfaction as a product of union negotiation for better working conditions rather than as a top-down gift from management. The unions believe that seniority is the appropriate method for upward movement toward less demanding, less dehumanizing, less tedious, and more rewarding jobs. They see "broad-banding"—i.e., allowing workers to do tasks outside of the strictly defined limits of their job descriptions—as a step toward reductions in the work force that will deprive employees of their jobs and unions of their members.

Actually, real gains can result from job restructuring if properly designed for the specific situation and implemented with the participa-tion of the workers and their representatives. Particular caution should be exercised to avoid both the jargon so precious to many behavioral scientists and management experts and the trap of unreal-istic expectations.

SUPERVISOR TRAINING

It is generally recognized that the key to effective management and the control of stress-provoking relationships within the organization is adequate training of first-line supervisors and middle-management personnel. Most organizations have supervisor-training programs, either developed in-house or purchased from one of the many firms offering prepackaged training materials or providing a contract training service. And yet, I am astonished to find how often this is done badly or not at all. Often, too much of the training deals with the technology of the work process and the keeping of records—important elements, to be sure—rather than with the human problems involved in managing people. These managerial functions, including decision-making, building teamwork, reducing stress, enforcing discipline relating to work rules, absenteeism, and behavior in the workplace, evaluating performance, criticizing or praising workers, handling complaints, and many more, have to be learned and, in many cases, periodically relearned. This requires training and indoctrination in language that the trainees can comprehend and with content that is not so general and theoretical that it has little relevance to the situations they face daily. Practice sessions involving role-playing exercises are useful learning devices in these programs.

A major part of the problem is the way supervisors are selected. The best workers don't always make the best supervisors and usually make poor ones when they spend so much time turning out work to keep the group's average from falling that they have little time left to devote to supervising others. In one large municipality where supervisors belong to the same union as the people they supervise, the desirable firm, fair, and consistent discipline that is so important to employee morale is virtually nonexistent. In one organization, the lack of strong management support has forced supervisors to surrender their authority to aggressively rowdy and rebellious employees.

Repeated studies have shown that supervisors and middle managers are more prone to stress-related health problems than any other level of the organizational hierarchy. This reflects the proverbial "double bind" of pressure from above as well as from below. Better training in performing their duties will relieve some of the stress, but inevitably much will remain. Accordingly, I would regard as incomplete any training program that does not school supervisors in coping with their own stress.

JOB DISCUSSION

This program involves a once- or twice-a-year meeting of an employee with his or her immediate supervisor to discuss the job, the way each relates to it and to each other, their attitudes and expectations, and any complaints. Although performance is invariably discussed, these meetings are not intended to focus on performance appraisal. Such meetings can be quite helpful in reducing stress if they are taken seriously by both parties, if some thinking is done prior to the meeting instead of allowing the discussion to be completely impromptu (although the discussion should be free-wheeling, a structured format for the agenda is quite helpful), and if the discussions can be honest, candid, and constructive without arousing resentment or provoking reprisal.

VARIABLE WORK SCHEDULES

Time pressure is one of the most prevalent stressors in the work setting. To ease the stress of rush-hour commuting in urban locations—and to reduce the risk of accidents in overcrowded subways and buses—many organizations have staggered hours so that the work force arrives in groups every fifteen or thirty minutes over a one- to two-hour period. Others have retained uniform starting and quitting times but have arranged with their neighbors to have each organization on a slightly different schedule.

Flextime is a modification that permits each individual to adjust work hours to suit his or her particular needs. Some organizations require that this be done on a regularly scheduled basis; others allow workers to come more or less as they please and leave when they have put in the required number of hours. Flextime tends to eradicate tardiness and the stress it creates for both the workers and their supervisors. It also enables employees to adjust to a train or bus schedule that gives them the alternative of arriving much too early or being late when on a "normal" schedule.

There are also a variety of modified work schedules: four-day weeks, three-day weeks, two-day week-ends alternating with three-day week-ends, etc. In some organizations, employees on "crash" assignments involving, for example, installing a piece of major equipment or a new computer program without interrupting continuing production, work around the clock until the job is done. They snatch catnaps on the premises when they have to and at the end are given compensatory time off for rest and relaxation.

At the Home Office of the Equitable Life Assurance Society, all of these different schedules are in use. The policy is that, as long as it is permitted by the flow of work and its relationship to the activities of other units or agencies outside the organization (e.g., customers, banks, and other financial institutions, the post office, government bureaus, etc.), the members of a unit may decide which schedule they would like. The rule is that, except for flextime, which can be individualized, all of the people in a unit must follow the modified schedule. A number of groups have tried a new schedule, only to elect to return to their earlier one when there were too many complaints.

These arrangements, supplemented by part-time work and shared jobs (i.e., two part-time employees combining to fill a single job), have allowed workers to resolve the conflict between their need to work and other demands on their time, such as family and community responsibilities, attending school, and recreational pursuits. This flexibility has permitted working parents to be at home when their children are not in school; this has been a particular boon to single parents in areas where day-care facilities are lacking.

These arrangements are not without problems. They create difficulty, for example, for supervisors who must monitor the activities of employees whose hours do not coincide with theirs. In more than one such situation, an overly conscientious supervisor was found to have extended his or her hours in order to continue to be the "first one in and the last one out." Car pools have been disrupted and two-career couples have been irked by work schedules that are markedly different. And then, there are individuals who have been bored and frustrated by having to enjoy their leisure time when "everyone else is working."

They have also presented problems to the organization. Employees have resented the imposition of a new schedule without having had a voice in planning the new arrangements. Some schedules with prolonged hours on fewer working days conflict with wage and hour regulations or union agreements, or lead to additional cost when overtime premiums are required even though the total hours for the week remain unchanged. Finally, there is an added burden on time keepers and personnel staff who must monitor attendance, and on telephone operators and others who must know when and where employees can be reached.

HEALTH EDUCATION AND PROMOTION

One of the more effective—and more frequently overlooked—mechanisms for preventing the adverse effects of stressors is educating employees to recognize the patterns they may display, teaching them to cope with high stress levels, and guiding them to the use of professional help when they need it. Rather than initiating a special program devoted exclusively to stress, it should be woven into the fabric of a more comprehensive program dealing with the varied aspects of occupational health and safety. It should also be explicitly included in all training programs, especially when introducing new processes and procedures.

Occupational safety and health regulations now require that employees be informed about potential hazards they may encounter on the job and be instructed in their avoidance and control. Concern over the increasing costs of health and disability benefits has prompted some organizations to initiate programs of preventive education and health promotion as one approach to containment of these costs. Yet, many organizations do little or nothing in this area.

Many reasons are given: The concept that health is a personal responsibility into which the organization should not intrude; the cost of designing and mounting an effective program; the apparent apathy of employees toward problems where there is such a lag between cause and effect; the perceived mistrust of employees of advice from management; and the fear of encouraging claims of work-related injury and disease. Perhaps the major reason is that the benefits of a health-education program are slow to appear and, because of the great number of intervening variables, difficult to measure. Acceptance of or indifference to the program is usually readily apparent. While it is quite simple to test cognition, the understanding and retention of the information, it is much more difficult to measure the extent to which the desired changes in attitudes and behavior occur.

Some argue that adulthood is too late for effective health education. By the time people are old enough to work, they contend, self-destructive attitudes and behavior have become deeply ingrained and inflexible. They would have preventive health education included as a substantial element in elementary and high school curriculae, when attitudes are still malleable and the hostility to authority that impels many people to ignore personal advice has not yet developed.

Yet, there is ample evidence that health-education programs do work. Much that is quoted is purely anecdotal, but there are many reports, too numerous to be discussed here, of controlled studies demonstrating desirable changes in life-style and work habits following involvement in a health-education program.

Examination of some of the more successful health-education programs suggests that attention should be paid to the following guidelines in introducing a program into work setting:

1 *The content of the program should be relevant.* While prepackaged materials should be used whenever possible—"reinventing the wheel" is costly and wasteful—they must be understood by and meaningful to the people for whom they are intended. The program should be tailored to the interests and perceived needs of the employees, and this may require programs of varying content for different segments of the work force.

2 *The program should be flexible.* It should be responsive to events and circumstances that may bring new concerns into prominence.

3 *The program should be interactive.* Purely didactic and exhortative approaches are much less effective than those that engage the participant in some kind of individual or group interaction.

4 *The program should not be based on fear or prejudice.* While cries of alarm are a good attention-getting device, it is well-established that the motivating effects of fear are short-lived. The exaggerated pejorative approaches that cater to prejudice which are so characteristic of certain advocacy groups and labor unions not only tend to wear thin but may actually boomerang and lead to a loss of credibility. Hazards should not be concealed; they should be exposed completely and realistically.

5 *The program should take full advantage of group dynamics and peer pressure.* Opportunity should be provided for small group meetings attended by trained discussion leaders or resource persons.

6 *Opportunity should be provided for individuals to get personalized information.* Individuals may be sensitive about certain subjects, and some may be reluctant to expose their ignorance about any topic. Resources to which employees can go for private, individualized answers to their questions should be made readily available and well publicized. It is not necessary that they be located in the work setting—for obvious reasons, community agencies may be preferable for this purpose—but advance arrangements should be made so

that employees will be received with a minimum of red tape and ceremony.

7 *Mechanisms should be included to involve employees' spouses and other family members.* It is not always feasible to invite family members to attend activities in the workplace, but because they are almost invariably involved in changing behavioral patterns, materials intended to enlist their active participation should be provided or even sent directly to the home.

8 *All information should be as accurate and up-to-date as possible.* All materials should be checked for completeness, clarity, and accuracy. When available, the relative advantages and disadvantages of alternative approaches to particular problems should be disclosed while fads and frauds should be decried.

9 *Employees should be involved in the design and modification of the program.* They are much more likely to value and participate in a program in which they have a sense of ownership. Union collaboration and endorsement will do much to enhance a program's acceptance.

10 *Mechanisms for evaluation of its effectiveness should be built into the program.* Continuing feedback leading to modification of the program is essential to its ongoing vitality.

Health education is a growing industry, and there are now many consultants and groups offering prepackaged programs or advice on designing and operating new ones. Voluminous catalogs listing health-education materials on all subjects and in all media are available. A most useful new wrinkle is provided by consultants who conduct training programs in which selected employees are taught to conduct health-education activities for their fellow workers. The recently created National Center for Health Education is an excellent source of information about the relative merits of various program elements and the qualifications of those offering help in program design and operation.

REFERENCES

Mitgang, H. (June 25, 1978). Behind the best sellers. *New York Times Book Review*, p. 52.

PART V
ORGANIZATIONAL CONSIDERATIONS

13

ACCIDENTS AND WORKER COMPENSATION AWARDS

Failure of the organization to recognize and control excessive levels of stress comes home to roost financially in terms of worker compensation costs. But increased premiums reflecting adverse experience are only part of the cost; they do not reflect loss of productivity due to downtime and damage to equipment.

Years ago, those individuals who had more than their share of accidents were referred to as "accident prone," and many studies were undertaken to define the characteristics by which they might be identified. Two groups were readily isolated: those who were in jobs that were clearly unsafe and those who were physically incapable of performing all of the tasks assigned to them. But these were accident-prone *situations,* not accident-prone *people.*

In detailed analyses of all of the personal factors related to the causation of accidents only one emerged as a common denominator: a high level of stress at the time the accident occurred. This is understandable when one recalls that the physiologic effects of stress include impaired concentration and attentiveness, slowed reaction time, and lessening of physical coordination. All these can be summarized in the axiom, "A person under stress is an accident about to happen."

In their classic studies of persons with more severe accidental injuries, Cleveland psychiatrists A. H. Hirschfeld and R. C. Behan (1966) confirmed the role of stress as a significant factor in causing the accident. They also found that, compounded by the stress produced by the injury, it tended to slow healing and both aggravate and prolong the disability. They demonstrated that by incorporating exploration and appropriate therapy of the sources of stress as early as possible into the treatment of the physical injuries, recovery was accelerated and residual disability reduced.

The precipitating and aggravating role of stress in accidental injury was known to health professionals for many decades before it was considered in the filing and adjudication of worker compensation claims. Under the no-fault concept embodied in all of the worker compensation laws and regulations,* the rate of stress was not considered material. An accident happened, physical impact occurred, and injury resulted. When emotional illness occurred following a physical injury, it was accepted as a part of the sequence and accepted as compensable. But claims based on injury following a stressful incident in which there was no direct physical contact were routinely denied. The classic case was the 1896 denial by the New York Court of Appeals of a claim for damages by a woman who attributed a miscarriage to the fright of a confrontation with some charging horses in which she was not physically touched (*Mitchell* v. *Rochester Railway Co.*, 1896).

By 1960, the courts began to award claims for physical disabilities resulting from occupational stress. For the most part, these were cases in which a heart attack or stroke was precipitated by a highly stressful episode at work. Although there were earlier examples, the one most frequently cited as the landmark case was *Klimas* v. *Trans-Caribbean Airway, Inc.*, in which the courts upheld an award to the widow of a thirty-three-year-old director of maintenance of the airline whose fatal heart attack was attributed to the extreme stress of his work. He had no history of heart disease; in fact, his heart had been found to be normal in a medical examination for a pilot's license eight months earlier. When one of the planes was grounded because of corrosion, the president of the airline accused him of being inept and he was constantly needled and harassed during the frustrating weeks it took to locate the needed spare parts and push the repairs. Then he was threatened with being fired unless he succeeded in negotiating a reduction in the bills for the repairs. At this point, he had his fatal attack. As one impartial

---

*   It should be noted that there is not only a lack of uniformity among the Worker Compensation laws and regulations in the fifty states and several federal jurisdictions, but there is also wide variation in the way they are interpreted in adjudicating disputed claims. When confronted by a problem case, the reader is cautioned to seek the advice of an attorney who is thoroughly familiar with those that are applicable to the particular situation.

specialist testified, "His anxiety was so great throughout, you didn't need much to push it over."

That remark illustrates the "last-straw" concept which guided decisions in such cases for many years. This requires evidence that an unusual episode or period of work-related stress, one significantly greater than the irritations to which the "average" worker in that job was "normally" subjected, was causally related to the injury on which the claim was based.

More recently, a new doctrine based on "repeated injury" has been introduced in California and has since spread to several other jurisdictions. This holds that the cumulative effects of repeated and continuous exposure to stress over an entire career can be held responsible for a heart attack or a stroke even though there had been no "unusual" episode.

All these cases involve instances of physical disease in which clinical evidence of damaged organs and tissues is demonstrable. Over the past twenty years, awards have been made with increasing frequency in cases in which work-related stress was claimed to have produced psychiatric illness and disability. Although far from the earliest, the one that received the most publicity was *Carter* v. *General Motors,* in which an assembly-line worker was awarded benefits for functional disability attributed to the accumulation of stress produced by his supervisor's criticism coupled with his inability to perform his job correctly.

The problem with these cases is the difficulty in measuring the kind and amount of stress involved. This is difficult enough to do when the victim is cooperative and all those involved have good memories. It is virtually impossible when the victim dies or is unable to be helpful. Since a decision must be rendered, the compensation referees and the courts are forced to rely on stereotypes and hearsay evidence. Because most worker compensation laws require that when there is uncertainty, the case must be decided in favor of the employee-claimant, the organization faces the extremely difficult task of proving that the employee's difficulty was *not* causally related to the stress of the job. While proof of the negative of such an issue is frequently impossible, the organization's case can sometimes be helped by evidence of its sensitivity to the problems of work-related stress and its provision of formal programs to deal with it.

However, since the impact of stress on the organization is far greater than even its potential liability for worker compensation awards, I would urge that these programs be aimed at really dealing with it rather than mere "window dressing" to bolster a disclaimer of financial responsibility for its effects.

REFERENCES

Carter v. *General Motors,* 1960 (106 NW 2d, 105).

Hirschfeld, A. H., and R. C. Behan (1966). The accident process. III. Disability: acceptable and unacceptable *J.A.M.A.* **197**:85–89.

Klimas v. *Trans-Caribbean Airways Inc.,* 1961 (207 NYS 2d 72).

Mitchell v. *Rochester Railway Co.,* 1896 (151 N.Y. 107).

14

EVALUATION
AND RESEARCH

Prudent management dictates that, just like every other aspect of an organization's operations, its programs and activities for dealing with work-related stress should be subjected periodically to critical and objective evaluation. Audit of the resources being applied and assessment of the results being achieved should lead to the decision to expand, contract, modify, eliminate, or simply continue the program.

Statements about "generally accepted principles of accounting," the constantly growing body of regulations promulgated by the Securities and Exchange Commission, and anecdotes about "creative" accounting attest to the difficulty in evaluating so seemingly prosaic a function as financial control. When, instead of dealing with such finite units as dollars and cents, one has to measure such abstractions as attitudes, behavior, and well-being, it is easy to see why organizations tend either to avoid these evaluations entirely or do them poorly. This does not, however, justify their neglect.

A proper evaluation addresses a number of critical questions:

1 *What is the mission of the program?* A definition of the purpose and specific goals of the program is fundamental to its initial design, and examination of their continuing applicability and relevance is a first step in the evaluation. In their interesting *Harvard Business Review* article, consultants David Sirota and Alan D. Wolfson (1973), using the analogy of the medical checkup, emphasize the importance of an accurate diagnosis that is reconfirmed regularly in trying to solve "people problems" in the organization.

2 *Is the program effectively designed and adequately staffed?* A seemingly constant characteristic of all programs is a tendency to inertia. Policies and procedures tend to accumulate in response to changing needs but there is often great resistance to "streamlining" by eliminating those that are obsolete and outmoded. Is the program design is appropriate? Is the staffing in terms of both time and capability inadequate, redundant, or sufficient? Attitudes of the staff should also be explored: Are they tired, jaded, or disinterested? Have they developed prejudices that hamper their capacity to relate to the people they serve?

3 *How well is the program working?* This focuses on the *process* of the program. Is it efficient and smooth? Are the procedures well performed and properly integrated? Is it impinging on employees' work time no more than is reasonable?

4 *How well is it being received?* Perhaps the best answer to this question lies in a study of the program's utilization. Is it reaching the people at whom it is aimed? It is being overutilized?

5 *What results is it producing?* Is the program accomplishing its mission? Are its benefits transient or long-lasting? Ideally, the program should make itself superfluous by eliminating completely the problem at which it was aimed.

6 *What is the cost-benefit ratio?* Given that the available resources in any organization are finite and that there are many unresolved problems, would they yield a better return if applied differently?

This is not the place for a detailed discussion of the methods of evaluation. I would merely emphasize the importance of good records and the utility of properly applied techniques of sampling and statistical analysis, and warn that, since much of the content of the problem and of the results is subjective, care must be exercised to be sure that the evaluation reflects the program rather than the preconceived notions of the evaluator.

Finally, I would stress, the evaluation should not be a sterile exercise. It should lead to concrete recommendations that will receive careful consideration from those responsible for the program. Not all may be currently feasible or politically acceptable, but if all change is foreclosed, there is no point in doing the evaluation.

Evaluation is a form of research. It is frequently useful to rewrite the report in a form suitable for publication in an appropriate scientific journal. While there may be nothing very earth-shaking in it, the presentation of the details of the program and a discussion of the results of the evaluation can be extremely useful to other organizations either as a model to emulate or as a warning to avoid repeating any mistakes. Sometimes the results will gain in significance by pooling them with those achieved by similar programs in other organizations.

Sometimes, the report can be made more meaningful by making the evaluation more comprehensive and collecting additional data. The decision will hinge on the interests of the evaluator as well as the availability of the resources required to do the extra work. I should point out that it may be possible to enlist outside help from a university or a research organization interested in the problem. I would urge as well that, whenever possible, the organization make itself and its work force available to qualified medical and social scientists for pure research; that is, research projects entirely independent of the periodic program evaluation. Despite the thousands of scientific publications on occupational stress, there remain many unanswered questions whose solutions can be found and tested only in the work setting. Some subjects can be studied in the isolation of a laboratory or the highly atypical environment of the university and some can be approached by the application of computer-modeling techniques, but the arena of the workplace is the only place where valid observations about human behavior in the world of work can be made.

CONCLUSION

As emphasized by the participants at the first World Health Organization Interdisciplinary Workshop on Psychosocial Factors and Health, which was held in Stockholm in October 1976, human beings should be regarded as entities constantly undergoing modification and being affected by their environments. Health problems can be related to one or more of a number of psychosocial mechanisms:

1 discrepancy between human needs and expectations and the means available for their satisfaction;

2 discrepancy between human capacities and the demands of a changing environment;

3 over- or understimulation by the environment;

4 role conflicts or incompatibility between the functions which individuals and groups are asked to perform;

5   the behavior of people with respect to unhealthy life-styles and their utilization of personal health services;

6   the insufficient attention to psychosocial factors in the management of work organizations and in the planning and delivery of health services; and

7   the dehumanization of societal institutions with respect to both the people who work in them and those whom they serve.

As emphasized repeatedly in the preceding chapters, these mechanisms operate as a continually varying network of influences. It is possible to focus on one and install a program or procedure that will modify its effects, but unless this is done within the context of all of the other current influences impinging on the individual or group, its benefits may be vitiated by problems that it creates. Just as there is no shortage of problems, there is no shortage of proposed solutions. Physicians and other providers of health services offer medical models of diagnosis and treatment but often focus too sharply on organs, functions, and medical technology, losing sight of the individual as an entity and remaining oblivious to his or her work role and its effect on his or her well-being. Psychologists postulate new theories and invent new forms of therapy which often can be opposed as cogently as they are proposed. Behavioral scientists analyze observations of small groups in special situations and extrapolate new formulas applicable everywhere. And, with considerable variation in marketing ability, all offer themselves and their programs to managers for use in their organization. The intent of this book is not to provide answers, but to enable the concerned manager to ask the right questions.

There is a need for more research into some of the basic assumptions about stress and its pathophysiology. We particularly need to be better able to comprehend the interplay between personal, work-related, and societal factors in the causation of breakdown. And, perhaps most of all, we need to bring together the varied disciplines, including management science, and force them to find a simple, jargon-free, common language to express their joint aspirations and to share their unique experiences.

REFERENCES

Sirota, D., and A. D. Wolfson (Jan.–Feb. 1973). Pragmatic approach to people problems. *Harvard Business Rev.* 51:120–128.

ADDITIONAL READING

Egdahl, R. H., and D. C. Walsh, eds. *Health Care Services and Health Hazards: The Employees Need to Know.* New York: Springer-Verlag, 1978.

_____. *Employee Mental Wellness Programs.* New York: Springer-Verlag, 1979.

Follman, J. P. *The Economics of Industrial Health: History, Theory, and Practice.* New York: Amacom, 1978.

Goldbeck, W. B. *A Business Perspective on Industry and Health Care.* New York: Springer-Verlag, 1978.

Kruzas, A. T., ed. *Medical and Health Information Directory.* Detroit: Gale Research Co., 1977.

Lawson, J. W., and J. W. R. Lawson. *Employee Absenteeism, Tardiness and Employee Morale.* Chicago: Dartnell Corp., 1973.

Levi, L. *Occupational Stress: Sources, Management, and Prevention.* Reading, Mass.: Addison-Wesley, 1979.

Levi, L., ed. *Society, Stress and Disease, Vol IV: Working Life.* London, New York, Toronto: Oxford University Press, 1979.

Levinson, H. *Emotional Health in the World of Work.* New York: Harper & Row, 1964.

_____. *Psychological Man.* Cambridge: The Levinson Institute, Inc., 1976.

Lusterman, S. *Industry Roles in Health Care.* New York: Conference Board, (Report No. 610), 1974.

McLean, A. A. *Work Stress.* Reading, Mass.: Addison-Wesley, 1979.

McLean, A. A.; G. Black; and M. Colligan; eds. *Reducing Occupational Stress.* Cincinnati: National Institute of Occupational Safety and Health, 1978. DHEW (NIOSH) Publication No. 78-140.

McLean, A. A., ed. *Mental Health and Work Organizations.* Chicago: Rand-McNally, 1970.

Marrow, A. J. *The Failure of Success.* New York: Amacom, 1972.

Moss, L. *Management Stress.* Reading, Mass.: Addison-Wesley, 1979.

Saltman, J. *Drinking on the Job.* New York: Public Affairs Committee (Pamphlet No. 544), 1977.

Selye, H. *Stress in Health and Disease.* Boston: Butterworths, 1976.

Shostak, Arthur B. *Blue-Collar Occupational Stress.* Reading, Mass.: Addison-Wesley, 1979.

Smirnow, B. W. *Industrial Programming for Mental Wellness: A Case Study Approach.* Washington, D.C.: Washington Business Group on Health, 1978.

Weiner H. J.; S. H. Akabas; and J. J. Sommer. *Mental Health Care in the World of Work.* New York: Association Press, 1973.

Wright, H. B. *Executive Ease and Disease.* New York: Halsted Press, 1975.

RESOURCES

The following comprise a partial listing of national organizations devoted to activities that may be included in stress-management programs, and of professional associations that can provide information about the roles their members may play in such programs, their qualifications for membership, and the credentials of a particular member.

Al-Anon Family Group
Headquarters and Alateen
P.O. Box 182
Madison Square Station
New York, N.Y.   10010

Alcoholics Anonymous
P.O. Box 459
Grand Central Station
New York, N.Y.   10017

American Academy of Psychoanalysis
40 Gramercy Park N.
New York, N.Y.   10010

American Association of Fitness
Directors in Business and Industry
400 Sixth Street, S.W., Suite 3030
Washington, D.C.   20201

American Association of Marriage and Family Counselors
41 Central Park West
New York, N.Y.   10023

American Examining Board of Psychoanalysis
80 Eighth Ave. Room 1210
New York, N.Y.   10011

American Health Foundation
320 East 43rd Street
New York, N.Y.   10017

American Institute of Stress
Tarrytown House
Executive Conference Center
East Sunnyside Lane
Tarrytown, N.Y.   10591

American Occupational Medical Association
150 N. Wacker Drive
Chicago, Ill.   60606

American Occupational Health Nurses Association
79 Madison Ave.
New York, N.Y.   10016

American Psychiatic Association
1700 18th Street N.W.
Washington, D.C.   20036

American Psychoanalytic Association
One East 57th St.
New York, N.Y.   10032

American Psychological Association
1200 17th Street N.W.
Washington, D.C.   20036

Association of Labor-Management
Administrators and Consultants on Alcoholism
1800 N. Kent Street (Suite 907)
Arlington, Va.   22209

Board of the National Registry of
Health Care Providers in Clinical
Social Work

1025 Dove Run Road
Lexington, Ky.   40502

Boston University
Center For Industry and Health Care
53 Bay State Road
Boston, Ma.   02215

Bureau of Health Education
Center for Disease Control
Department of Health, Education and Welfare
1600 Clifton Road, N.E.
Atlanta, Ga.   30333

Canadian Health Information Directorate
Tunney's Pasture
Ottawa, Ontario, KIA OK9

Department of Health Education
American Medical Association
535 North Dearborn Street
Chicago, Ill.   60610

High Blood Pressure Information Center
120/80
National Institutes of Health
Bethesda, Md.   20014

National Association of Social Workers
1425 H. Street N.W.
Washington, D.C.   20005

National Center for Health Education
211 Sutter Street
San Francisco, Ca.   94108

National Clearinghouse for Alcohol Information
Alcohol, Drug Abuse and Mental Health Administration
P.O. Box 2345
Rockville, Md.   20852

National Clearinghouse for Drug Abuse Information
Alcohol, Drug Abuse and Mental Health Administration
5600 Fishers Lane, Room 10-A56
Rockville, Md.   20857

National Clearinghouse for Mental Health Information
National Institute of Mental Health
5600 Fishers Lane
Rockville, Md.   20857

National Council on Alcoholism
733 Third Avenue
New York, N.Y.   10017

National Institute for
Occupational Safety and Health
5600 Fishers Lane
Rockville, Md.   20857

National Safety Council
444 North Michigan Avenue
Chicago, Ill.   60611

Office for Handicapped Individuals
Department of Health, Education and Welfare
338 D Hubert Humphrey Building
200 Independence Avenue, S.W.
Washington, D.C.   20201

Office of Health Information and Promotion
Department of Health, Education and Welfare.
721 B Hubert Humphrey Building
200 Independence Avenue, S.W.
Washington, D.C.   20201

President's Council on Physical Fitness and Sports
400 Sixth Street, S.W. Room 3030
Washington, D.C.   20201

Provide Addict Care Today/National Association
on Drug Abuse
355 Lexington Avenue
New York, N.Y.   10017

Washington Business Group on Health
605 Pennsylvania Avenue, S.E.
Washington, D.C.   20003

Y's Way to a Healthy Back Program
Pacific Region YMCA
3080 La Selva
San Mateo, Ca.   94403

INDEX